The Courage To
Rise

Praise For *The Courage To Rise*

"Charmaine has done something truly incredible. She has not only identified the challenges that come with loving and being loved fully. She has laid out for those wandering in the deserts of isolation the barriers set up that keep love out, and the keys to remove them. More than that, Charmaine reminds us that, despite the tumult or trauma of the past, letting love in is indeed possible."

—**Dr. Nicole Bossard**, President and Positivity Strategist, TGC Consulting Inc.

"*The Courage To Rise* is an authentic and honest journey into discovering the barriers that keep us all from experiencing all we can from love. Charmaine's storytelling and connections are disarming and bold. A soul stirring composition of love.

—**BCR**, advocate, educator, doula, and feminist

"This book is the antonym of a scarcity mindset when it comes to love. When Heard encourages the reader to 'rise in love' she doesn't mean 'reach for what is outside of you,' she means for you to stand up tall in the abundance that has always been there inside of you, just misrecognized because of a litany of obstacles (psychological, trauma induced, emotional) that have simply been blocking the view. With extraordinary gentleness and care, Heard is taking your hand and walks you through the steps it takes to let go of those obstacles to self love, and deepen a serious practice of radical loving-kindness both toward yourself and the world."

—**Dr. Michael Washington**, lecturer in critical studies

MY PERSONAL QUEST TO HAPPY, HEALTHY LOVE

The Courage To Rise

*How To Transform
The Barriers That
Hold Us Back From
Healthy Relationships
And Real Love*

Charmaine Heard

INDIE BOOKS
INTERNATIONAL

The Courage To Rise
How To Transform The Barriers That Hold Us Back From Healthy Relationships And Real Love

No part of this publication may be reproduced or distributed in any form or by any means, without the prior permission of the publisher. Requests for permission should be directed to permissions@indiebooksintl.com, or mailed to Permissions, Indie Books International, 2511 Woodlands Way, Oceanside, CA 92054.

The views and opinions in this book are those of the author at the time of writing this book, and do not reflect the opinions of Indie Books International or its editors.

Neither the publisher nor the author is engaged in rendering legal or other professional services through this book. If expert assistance is required, the services of appropriate professionals should be sought. The publisher and the author shall have neither liability nor responsibility to any person or entity with respect to any loss or damage caused directly or indirectly by the information in this publication.

Disney® is a registered trademark of Disney Enterprises, Inc.

TED® is a registered trademark of Ted Conferences, LLC

YouTube® is a registered trademark of Google, LLC

Jenga® is a registered trademark of Pokonobe Associates

Barbie® is a registered trademark of Mattel, INC.

Teflon® is a registered trademark of The Chemours Company FC, LLC

Goldfish® is a registered trademark of Pepperidge Farms, Incorporated

FaceTime® is a registered trademark of Apple, Inc.

Lyrics from "I See Thoughts" are used with permission from Toni Jones and I Am Music Group Incorporated.

ISBN 13: 978-1-966168-44-7
Library of Congress Control Number: 2025920523

Cover art by Ann Lam-Anh Pham.
Designed by Melissa Farr, Back Porch Creative, LLC

INDIE BOOKS INTERNATIONAL®, INC.
2511 WOODLANDS WAY
OCEANSIDE, CA 92054
www.indiebooksintl.com

To my younger self,
You are my favorite—I love you.
I will continue learning how to love you best
and will always be your greatest friend.

Contents

Prologue

Owning our story can be hard but not nearly as difficult as spending our lives running from it.
BRENÉ BROWN

I finally had enough strength to sit up in my bed. My eyes were swollen, and my head was pounding from what seemed like hours of crying. My first thought was, "I'm not going to make it to December."

That was in June 2021. My husband, Rick, had died unexpectedly the month prior. I was overwhelmed with grief and stress. From the moment I received the news of his death until a week after his funeral, my adrenaline was in high gear.

The adrenaline was how I was able to plan and execute his funeral. It carried me through, even though during that entire time, I was holding a tremendous amount of pain, hurt, confusion, and fear throughout my body. Those feelings had been living inside me for some time prior to his death, but they intensified to a level I was sure I could not withstand. His death was untimely, and for me, it happened at the worst possible stage in our marriage.

Rick and I were separated when he passed away. I would have never predicted that our love story would end this way. Our separation was no reflection on the deep love I had for him. It felt unfair that it had ended the way it did. Now, any hope I had for us was gone. I knew my life would never be the same. But I had no way of knowing just how much my life was about to change.

Following Rick's funeral, all I wanted to do was talk to my Grandma Gray. I wanted to hold her hand while we sat in silence on her couch. I wanted to hear her voice and words of wisdom. I wanted to cry on her shoulder. She was a safe harbor for me. I knew I was loved by her no matter what.

However, I couldn't sit with her because she had passed away four months before Rick. I was grieving her death as well. I was deeply saddened that two of the most significant loves of my life died within months of each other.

My dear father-in-law, with whom I shared a kind love, had also died ten months prior to Rick's passing. I was missing him as well.

Now, sitting up, I slid back against my headboard, tilted my head back, and placed my hands on my heart. I began doing a breathing meditation in hopes that it would ease the pain in my head. I was also trying to slow down all of the thoughts that were swirling in my head.

It took some time, but I felt myself settle into a calm state. In that calm state, a passage from the book *Daring Greatly* by Dr. Brené Brown popped into my head.

"The Man In The Arena"
by Theodore Roosevelt

It is not the critic who counts; not the man who points out how the strong man stumbles, or where the doer of deeds could have done them better. The credit belongs to the man who is actually in the arena, whose face is marred by dust and sweat and blood; who strives valiantly; who errs, who comes short again and again, because there is no effort without error and shortcoming; but who does actually strive to do the deeds; who knows great enthusiasms, the great devotions; who spends himself in a worthy cause; who at the best knows in the end the triumph of high achievement, and who at the worst, if he fails, at least fails while daring greatly, so that his place shall never be with those cold and timid souls who neither know victory nor defeat.

Brown's teaching has been a source of encouragement over the years. She taught me to dare greatly, rise strongly, and brave the wilderness, with all my imperfections in tow.

Roughly thirty minutes into my meditation, the pain in my head eased.

I stretched, reached over, and grabbed the book, *A Course of Love* by Mari Perron, a book my therapist recommended. Chapter 20, "Wholeheartedness—The Embrace," was where I had left off. The words in that chapter leapt off the pages and straight into my heart. I felt love was literally holding me through that entire chapter. The sentence that summed it all up for me in the chapter was, "Love is all that matters because love is all that is."[1]

Peace, comfort, and renewed hope settled in me for the first time since the day Rick transitioned. I pulled out my journal, which I keep next to my bed, and began to write. That journal entry turned into me making commitments to myself.

I committed to allowing myself to take an honest assessment of my life. I promised myself that I would feel every emotion that came up for me instead of stuffing them away, even completely falling apart if I had to. I committed to allowing love to show me how to come back to a place of wholeness because I felt like I was broken into a million pieces.

My last commitment was that I would make something beautiful out of this seemingly hard, messy, and painful life for as long as I'm on this earth by loving myself and others well with all that I have.

For over ten years, I have been exploring the idea of love and healthy relationships. Maybe I watched too many Disney movies as a little girl, but I wanted to live out a great love story, too.

My exploration of love turned into a mission, a quest, if you will, to experience real love and to be in healthy relationships. I felt that I hadn't come into the full experience of love yet. There was always a feeling I had inside that there was something more.

During this quest, I've fallen short so many times that I wanted to throw in the towel. But I would always feel a gentle nudge. I'd hear a calm, steady voice encouraging me to get up, dust myself off, and move forward.

Sometimes, that voice would tell me to just rest. Somehow, I regained the stamina to rise and take the next step forward.

The hardship I faced in 2021 wasn't the first time things had fallen apart for me but it was the catalyst to healing some deep wounds I was still carrying. After making those commitments to myself, I decided to step away from any distractions that would keep me from working on myself. I chose to spend the majority of my time alone for almost two years, learning and healing.

This was my chance to go all in for love. I was determined to figure out how to live the life I'd always dreamed of for myself. At times, I had to walk through uncharted terrain, trying to navigate through some of the lessons I needed to learn.

But like the saying goes, when the student is ready, the teacher will appear. Each time I thought I was stuck, the right person came along to help me. Whether it was my coaches, my therapists, an author, a friend, a family member, or a YouTube video, it was perfect timing.

We all will face hardship, setbacks, and losses throughout our lives. What matters is how we come back from those experiences; what we do next matters. All of the great leaders and my ancestors faced far greater hardships and losses, yet they kept going. If they'd found the strength to keep going, so could I.

As I share my journey of rising in love, one of the healthiest things I've learned was the art of letting go while keeping love intact. I am letting go of wanting a specific outcome, including how well this book will be received.

I learned to let go of relationships that were unhealthy for me and still stand in love for myself and others. This statement isn't past tense—I'm still learning how to let go. Deeply connecting with others is nourishing to me, so relationships matter to me. There is a bit of a recovery period I go through when a relationship changes. Learning to let go has been one of the hardest practices of my life.

I've found that there is freedom in letting go, not just mine but for all involved. And I've learned to accept when others have decided to let me go as well. What's amazing is that letting go opens room for other beautiful relationships to blossom. So, my story continues.

The Optimist

To know genuine love is to invest time and commitment.
BELL HOOKS

I've had this insatiable curiosity about life and people since I was a young girl. To be more specific, my curiosity is about love and human connection. It fascinates me; it's perplexing too.

Throughout my life I was constantly hearing people say life is hard and painful. I would be warned that I would be let down if I had any expectations that other people would do right by me. I felt this sense of resignation in people to accept and expect poor behaviors of others.

Accepting this standard of life was just not going to work for me. It's like we were made to believe we are supposed to be in hell on earth. Here's what I was told: "People are awful, Charmaine. You better be lucky to have what you have because the world is not a nice place. Expect to be hurt because that is what people do."

But the thing is, I'm strong-willed and I have a bit of a stubborn streak in me. So, I refuse to accept as a life sentence that I won't have loving, healthy relationships. I do believe in the goodness of humanity.

Don't get me wrong, I've questioned it on numerous occasions, but I come back to the same conclusion. People do awful things, yes. But there's a lot of goodness to experience with some truly wonderful people.

I know I'm up to risky behavior here. I've risked my heart and got it crushed many times over. There were people who risked loving me, and I hurt their hearts as well. And for that, I am willing to do better every single day.

Choosing the path of love and healthy relationships is not what I thought it would be at the beginning of this journey. I've had to unlearn and learn new ways of relating. I've had to stand alone at times. I've had to stand in the face of hurt and pain. But along the way, I discovered that there's a fierceness to love, too.

All of the great leaders of love that I've learned from have harnessed a great deal of bravery. They risked being strange in society, being ousted by their community, and even losing their lives for love. If there's one thing we should never have to lose our lives believing in, love would be that one thing.

To love well is my nod to all who came before me. I will help carry the torch forward in honor of all that is. Mahatma Gandhi encouraged us to forge ahead by being the change we want to see in the world. That's where it all started for me: becoming more of what I want to see and experience.

My Aha Moment

Even before I graduated from college, I landed a job with a member-owned and member-governed organization and excelled at it. That job was followed by others at the vice president and director levels. As I grew in my career, however, I had an ongoing and pressing urge to learn about healthy relationships and love, which was sparked fifteen years ago.

In 2010, I received my first coaching certification from the Institute for Integrative Nutrition (IIN). I initially attended this program in New York City to learn how to live more holistically. I had been diagnosed with high blood pressure and polycystic ovary syndrome. I wanted to address those issues because I was planning to one day start a family with Rick. I had no idea that my pressing urge and curiosity about love and relationships were about to be ignited.

It was during one of our Saturday sessions inside the Lincoln Center. The instructor explained that we live off of primary and secondary foods. "The food we eat is actually secondary. Your primary food is made up of healthy relationships, regular physical activity, a fulfilling career, and spiritual practice. We are not only fed by food but also by the energy in our lives," he explained.

The instructor's explanation was my first huge aha moment—so much so that I wanted to leap out of my chair with excitement. I looked around to see if others were moved the same way I was, but no one else seemed fazed by it. While my peers in the program were planning for coaching practices in nutrition and exercise, I chose to follow the primary foods thread, particularly healthy relationships, since that is what both intrigued and eluded me.

Following my graduation from IIN, I started reading everything I could get my hands on about love, healthy relationships, and whole-person healing. I watched videos, read books, and listened to podcasts from thought leaders about these topics.

While I was still working full-time, I started a small business centered around romantic relationships. It seemed easy enough to begin there because I thought Rick and I had it down pat in that area and could inspire others. However, I couldn't base love just on what I thought or experienced, so I came up with the idea of interviewing couples about their relationships and posting articles with their stories as inspiration.

During the interviews, I was always impressed with the close relationships I heard about. But it wasn't long, however, before a few couples began contacting me to request that their articles be taken down because their relationships were ending for various reasons.

I decided to stop interviewing couples altogether. Many of the couples that I interviewed, however, are still doing well together.

After serious contemplation, I wondered if our own inner journey toward wholeness might determine the health of our relationships. Maybe relationships are as healthy or unhealthy as the individuals in the relationship. My exploration turned down the path of self-love.

Here We Go!

Love is a form of sweet labor: fierce, bloody, imperfect, and life-giving—a choice we make over and over again. If love is sweet labor, love can be taught, modeled, and practiced.
—VALARIE KAUR

When I first started down this path of self-love, I had no idea where to go, how to do it, or what was going to come out of it. "Begin where you are," my life coach Ed told me, and so I did.

I recognized that I had privilege when it came to figuring this out. Not everyone has access to the resources, methods, or people that could help. This work was never just for me. As I studied and put into practice what I was learning, I shared my insights with others to inspire and encourage them to find their paths as well.

My hope was that some of the things I learned could also help others along the way. Healthy relationships aren't something we are taught in school. Healing through pain and hurt is not openly discussed. As a matter of fact, it is not socially acceptable to do that.

The practice of healing and restoring ourselves to wholeness when there is hurt is vital. My argument for why is that if we don't address our pain and work on healing those wounds and scars, we end up throwing our unresolved pain on those around us, inflicting more pain on ourselves and others.

I can see that my own experiences and past hurts prevented me from living peacefully with others. I couldn't experience relationships the way I wanted to because I was still holding on to some painful times in my life. I was also repeating the same patterns from my past, which resulted in the same outcome, just with different people, especially in friendships. I knew I couldn't do this alone; I needed help.

As a love nerd, I spent time gathering as much data as I could from thought leaders around the world. What I'd gathered early on is that real love begins with learning how to love ourselves well, nurturing that love, and being brave enough to allow ourselves to heal the wounded parts of ourselves. It's a practice. Practicing real love happens both with our individual selves and in relationships with others.

> ... real love begins with learning how to love ourselves well, nurturing that love, and being brave enough to allow ourselves to heal the wounded parts of ourselves. It's a practice. Practicing real love happens both with our individual selves and in relationships with others.

I didn't need to disappear and figure it out and then come back. I used to think I had to go away and "fix" myself before resuming my relationship with others. Thankfully, I learned that it's in relationships with others that I learn how well I'm doing in love.

One of the pressing questions I had was, "How do other people define love?"

One of the pressing questions I had was, "How do other people define love?"

I needed to figure out how I could gather data that would give me context and understanding. That data could help me learn how to love more and love better. This was based on my novice assumption that we aren't doing well in love.

If you've been around me long enough, you know about the love boards. I got custom-made chalkboards so that people could write what love means to them. I captured their answers by taking a picture. I collected data on what they shared. Some of my friends joined in to help me.

Those boards have been all over the US and parts of the world. Some people shared their personal stories about love with me. Those boards caught a lot of tears as people wrote their answers. As I look back, that was such a beautiful experience for me. It was a gift to meet so many strangers, yet we had a brief connection over the idea of love.

This little movement opened the door for me a few years later. I began receiving invitations to speak at nonprofits, businesses, schools, and government agencies.

As my interest in healthy relationships, love, and personal growth grew, my interest in my other career lessened. I didn't know how to reconcile my budding fascination with this work and keep a career that was no longer interesting to me.

From the very beginning of our relationship, I made an agreement to always make life really good for Rick. I didn't want him to want for anything if I could help it. The memory that sticks with me the most from our wedding day was when I was sitting alone in the limo waiting to walk down the aisle. I said to myself, "Charmaine, your job is to make that man so happy for the rest of his life." I believed he deserved to live a great life. I set out to center him in my life and marriage. I now understand this was the wrong approach to a healthy marriage.

With all due respect, since he is no longer with us, what I share is from my experience and perspective. My passion for healthy, happy relationships is a part of the legacy I want to leave in honor of our marriage, as imperfect as it was. I loved him the best way I knew how. Only he and I truly know the truth about what happened between us.

It seemed Rick was comfortable with the life we had, but around year fourteen, I was growing unhappy and stressed, although not about us specifically. I was burnt out from my corporate job. I couldn't keep it all together. Tension between Rick and me heightened, and we hadn't built the skills needed to resolve our differences.

Rick and I didn't fight or raise our voices at each other. Not having the skills to deal with our breakdowns was damaging to the relationship. It was hard for me to know because he didn't share his true thoughts or feelings with me. I felt left in the dark. For our entire marriage, I tried not to upset him. We were conflict-avoidant, it seems. We both share responsibility for that.

It's Time To Heal And Grow

Your task is not to seek for love, but merely to seek and find all the barriers within yourself that you have built against it.

Rumi

Years ago, I read the quote attributed to the Sufi poet Rumi. His statement intrigued me. The intriguing part was the idea that barriers are holding me back from experiencing love fully.

I came across similar teachings from thought leaders who were saying the same thing. Jesuit priest Anthony De Mello puts it this way, in his book *The Way to Love*, "Understand the obstructions you are putting in the way of love, freedom, and happiness, they will drop."[2] Michael A. Singer is another leader of love who shares a similar message.

I decided to challenge Rumi, De Mello, and Singer's theory. I was going to explore all the ways I am blocking (obstructing) love, freedom, joy, and healthy relationships for that matter. It wasn't a question of whether I had barriers; it was about understanding what they were, why I had created them, and how to remove them.

The game plan was to identify the barriers, understand them, recognize unhealthy patterns, establish healthy new patterns of behavior, and understand how I could relate to others from a healthier perspective.

This book will capture some of my personal journey, my quest to find the courage to rise and keep going. My relationship with Rick has been the most significant (romantic) relationship to date, so I will touch on it as it relates to the barriers.

I will share how the areas of holding on to the past, lack of self-care, lack of integrity, dishonesty, lack of emotional safety, resentment, forgiveness, boundaries, fear, comparison, criticism, and the need for approval were some of the barriers I addressed first. There are others, but this is where I started. These barriers were erected in response to experiences throughout my life. The experiences influenced how I have shown up in marriage, friendships, work, and my community.

In the next section, I will provide some background about my life and then share the work I've done in each of these areas.

When I set out to write this book, I wondered who this book would be for. I wrote this book for me, this work was getting to my own salvation. It's also for the person who is on their own personal journey to the greatest love they could imagine for themselves—the person who is willing to keep going no matter what gets thrown at them. It is for that one person courageous enough to bet on themselves by rising to love, in order to experience inner peace and freedom. It's for us.

My intention is to offer you a perspective that perhaps there are barriers that may be blocking the happy, healthy, and loving relationships you desire. Maybe dismantling the barriers will transform your relationship with yourself and others, allowing love to flow. As you read this book, I empower you to allow your inner compass to guide you.

It is courageous to actually allow yourself to be the powerful loving human you were born to be. May this book inspire you to live an even more authentic, beautiful life, no matter what. May your own journey inspire you.

The Foundation

"Poetry Is Not A Luxury"
by Audre Lorde

If what we need to dream, to move our spirits most deeply and directly toward and through promise, is discounted as a luxury, then we give up the core—the fountain—of our power, our womanness; we give up the future of our worlds.

There I was lying flat on my back in the grass, staring into the clear blue sky, letting my mind wander, dreaming away. That was until I heard my grandmother yell out to me, "Girl, get up off the ground like that before the chiggers bite you." I slowly stood up and reoriented myself back to my surroundings.

I was in the front yard of my maternal grandparents' house. Looking around, I saw my cousins playing. Some played basketball while others rode their bikes or played with their Barbie dolls. There was a light rhythm and harmony in view.

Grandma was right, I was itchy from the bites I had gotten lying in the grass, but I didn't mind because lying there offered such peace. I felt at home with myself for that short time. I was nine years old then. Many years later, I still find myself lying on my back staring at the blue sky and sometimes the moon and stars too. It's my way of finding myself at home again. It also gives me the chance to continue dreaming.

I've always been a dreamer. At nine, I had quite an imagination, so I dreamed about how fun life was and the adventures I would take. By the time I was a teenager, I was dreaming about being an actress, musician, and spending time with a cute boy I was crushing on at the time. As a young adult, I dreamt of traveling the world as a performer, enjoying life, and having gatherings with lots of food and fun with my beloved, my family and friends.

Around the age of nineteen, it became harder for me to dream. Life's challenges got in the way of that. But the rare times I allowed myself to, I dreamt of a life where my friends, family, and the man I was lucky enough to love would move in that light rhythm and harmony of my childhood. We would gather for delicious meals, play games, travel, dance, and enjoy great music together. In all of my dreams, we were all safe, relaxed, happy, loved, and free.

Family

Although I am my parents' only child, I had the experience and blessing of being raised in a multigenerational home until the age of eleven. During those years, I lived with my maternal grandparents, my mom, her sisters, her brother, and my cousins. There were at least fifteen of us living together at any given time. My maternal great-grandmother, who owned the eight acres of land on which we lived, was just a few yards away. My eldest aunt and her children lived with my great-grandmother.

There were a lot of people to share space with, so I learned to live in community with others from birth. Experience truly is the greatest teacher, as I learned how to navigate all types of personalities while living at Grandma's house. It taught me how to accept people for who they are. The seed for acceptance of diversity was planted early and would bloom more in my adult life.

My grandparents shared their values with us, but we didn't all apply them in the same way.

An adult was always around to look after my cousins and me. We also looked after each other. My aunts pitched in to help get me ready for school or bed when my mom was at work. I didn't mind my aunts helping me before school, unless it was Aunt Abby. She did my hair in the one style I didn't like every time. She styled my hair for my fifth-grade class photo, so it will always be a part of my personal history. If I had children of my own, that would be one of the (now) funny stories I would share with them.

My cousins were my first friends. We woke up together, got ready for school together, played together, and ate all our meals together. Grandma would hand us our plates in the kitchen, and we would then take a seat at the dining room table, wait for everyone else to be seated, and say our grace together. Most nights felt like a slumber party.

Of course, there were plenty of arguments, disagreements, and fights. How could there not be? Things got intense at times. I got in more trouble than most of my cousins because I talked back a lot and was defiant. The beauty of it was that we learned how to come back together after those rough moments, albeit maybe with some hurt feelings and scars.

No matter what stage of life I was in, my maternal grandparents' house was always my home base. When the world didn't feel right, their house was a respite for me. It was the place I knew I was loved, I belonged, and I was safe.

While my maternal grandparents (Julius and Florence) played a significant role in my understanding of love, belonging, and safety, I experienced that with three other grandparents and three great-grandparents as well. Florence's mother (Evelyn), my paternal grandmother (Lilian), her husband (Ernest), Lilian's parents (Charlie and Edna), and my paternal grandfather (Morris) were all positive influences in my life.

As I reflect on the time shared with each of them, I realize how lucky I was to know them. From braiding Great-Grandma Edna's hair while listening to her talk about her life, to talking to Pop Charlie outside by the clothesline as the chickens ran around, to snapping peas with Great-Grandma Evelyn and listening to her life stories (she had the most beautiful smile), to meeting Grandaddy Morris at my surprise twenty-fifth birthday party and getting to spend one-on-one time with him. Their presence was a gift.

I have countless memories with Julius and Florence, whom the grandchildren called Grandaddy and Grandma (Gray), because I lived with them. One of my fondest memories with Julius is our nightly family prayers. He gathered all of the grandchildren before bed in his room and prayed for us. We giggled every night while he prayed for each of us one by one. As for Florence, we could often find her wearing her apron, working on a puzzle, reading the Bible, or watching one of her old black-and-white "pictures," her term for old Western shows.

Fortunately, I am still able to make more memories with Lilian, who's now ninety-two years old, and Ernest, who's now eighty-four years old, because they're both still here with me.

Julius was the one who made the biggest impact on my young life. He had this expansive capacity to love all of us. In his masculinity, Julius had a depth of care, generosity, and kindness that felt unique and special. The way he loved and respected my grandma as the matriarch of our family was life-giving.

My grandaddy was a man of many words. He had the gift of gab. When I was in trouble and my grandaddy wanted to talk to me, I would start crying. He was the one person I didn't want to disappoint because he was so loving to everyone. He never spanked me. His very long lectures were punishment enough. I'm sure there was a lot of wisdom in what he was saying, but my listening skills as a young kid were horrible.

It wasn't what he said that made an impact on me; it was his actions. The way he showed up for his wife and family was love. My granddaddy was strong. He didn't hide his vulnerabilities from us. He was the one I could go to with anything. Even if he was disappointed by something I did, he firmly let me know, yet held compassion for me at the same time.

Along with my grandparents, my parents raised me as well. In addition to my mom, Sheila, and my dad, Lawerence, I also had stepparents: Mark, my mom's husband, and Rosemary, my dad's wife. Yes, my family tree has many branches.

My biological parents were in their late teens when I came along. They were still growing up themselves. As you can imagine, there were lots of learning curves as to how to be parents and live their young lives.

I have some fond memories with them, as well as painful ones. On my journey, healing my relationship with them has changed me forever. It took me years to come to a place of peace. I now have a better relationship with them.

What I know for sure is that they love me the best way they know how, and for that I am thankful. I am free to love them. I no longer need them to fix the parts of my childhood that were hard for me.

Working on the barriers helped me heal those relationships. My parents, all four of them, were there for me when things got really tough. I'm not the easiest only child. I'm super independent. I tend to lean toward taking care of everything myself without asking for help.

They were there for me when it mattered most. I see their goodness at the core of it all. I'm grateful that I came to this place now and can share life with them from a place of love while we are all still here. It is not perfect by any means, but mending my relationship with them is a miracle.

We will never be perfect at this, but my commitment is to continue to rise in love. There are times when I still need to deal with my ego. But love will take you on an incredible journey if you're willing to take the ride.

Age Eleven

When I turned eleven, some big changes unsettled my foundation of security. I went through a rough patch during my middle school years. Life as I knew it was changing, starting with my body. I was developing hips and breasts. I had periods and pimples.

Not only was my body changing, but my physical living space changed, too. I moved in full-time with my mom and new stepfather; it was a drastic change. I went from a house with an average of fifteen people to a house of three. We moved to my stepfather's childhood home, a county north of my family, about twenty-five minutes away. To me, it felt like hours away.

Although I went to my grandparents' every day before and after school, my life wasn't the same.

My stepfather's house was very old and was directly across from a cemetery. I was told it used to be a schoolhouse for Black children. To the right of the house, up the hill through the sparse woods, was a small church. On the left were a few school buses and uncultivated land. It was a lonesome street with a few houses. It was so unlike the acres of land at my grandparents' house, with neighbors and other children to play with.

I can picture my eleven-year-old self, standing just inside the doorway of my new bedroom, where all of my belongings now lived, too. The room was sizable and oddly shaped for a bedroom. In the first section of my bedroom, there was a bed with lots of room for my stuffed animals, dollhouse, dolls, and books, so I set up shop for them there. The second section of the room contained the bed I slept in, a huge closet, my stereo equipment, a television, and a dresser.

Another bedroom next to mine on the first floor was even bigger. We used that bedroom to iron clothes and store extra stuff. My mom and stepfather stayed in one of the three bedrooms upstairs. It took me some time to adjust to all the changes.

I had to figure out how to live as an only child. The house was so quiet compared to what I was used to. I had to entertain myself, cook for myself at times, and clean the whole house. I had new house rules.

And I had to learn how to be home alone sometimes because, as I mentioned, there was always someone around at Grandma's house. I wasn't used to being alone for extended periods of time.

The first time I woke up and my parents were gone, I panicked. It was a Saturday morning. I didn't hear them moving about. My stepfather hadn't knocked on my door to wake me up to do my chores, as he usually did. When I called out for my mom, she didn't answer. I was too scared to move. It took me a long time to get up and look for them. They were gone.

I was convinced that the second coming of Christ, the rapture, had come, and I was left behind. I may have been dramatic, but it was so real to me at the time. When my mom and stepfather arrived home, I wanted to hug my mom and ask her, please, not to leave me alone again, but I played it cool. I was scared to show how I really felt. I didn't want to cause any problems or get in trouble for being dramatic.

Being alone in that house was my first real lesson in facing my fears and thinking on my feet. On Saturdays, random strangers would knock on the door when I was home alone. I would tell them my parents were busy and couldn't come to the door. I was afraid, but tried not to let them see it.

Once, an old white man with a long gray beard and a weird lump protruding from his neck knocked at the door. I peeked out and jumped back. He asked if I was home alone, and I said no. I was lying. He proceeded to ask me to open the door, but I didn't. He attempted several times to open the door but realized he couldn't get in.

From that moment on, I felt even more unsafe. It didn't help that we were robbed while living at that house, too.

I began acting out my feelings of being a scared child. Life got so confusing to me. I talked back a lot, got in fights, was difficult with my family, and was just plain stubborn. I had a hard time focusing in middle school. My grandfather, Julius, was aware of what was happening. I could see the disappointment in his face. After a while, he had had enough. He sat down one-on-one with me and let me know he was not OK with my behavior.

While his demeanor was calm, it was clear he was serious. This time, he had my full attention. Once Julius realized that I got the message, he ended our very long conversation with great compassion and grace. He shared that he understood that things may be hard for me, but everything was going to be OK. He knew why I was acting out, but he wasn't going to let me get away with it.

After that discussion, I cleaned up my act. I am forever grateful that Julius Gray set me straight. That conversation perhaps changed the direction of where my life was going.

Getting good grades, preparing for college, and staying out of trouble became my focus. My creativity and independence blossomed by participating in school activities and learning to entertain myself at home. I began cultivating a love for reading, music, writing, television, and movies. Life opened up for me with every story and lyric I heard.

I was a sponge soaking in as much as I could. My imagination grew, but it was in such conflict with my reality. My parents kept me in church. They had some pretty strict rules based on the religion they practiced.

Around the age of eleven my grandfather Julius had a stroke. The left side of his body was paralyzed. It took years but thankfully he regained a lot of his motion back. About ten years later, Julius had complications with diabetes.

A week before he passed away, he was sitting on the couch in the living room. It was the couch where he and my grandmother sat at night and held hands as they watched television together. Other family members were around but I can only recall my grandmother being near him. I heard talking but I wasn't really listening.

I looked at Julius, this beautiful dark-skinned man who was my granddaddy. He was looking back at me and, without saying anything, I understood what he was saying. He was acknowledging that he wasn't going to be here much longer and that he loved me. I lowered my gaze because my heart began to ache, and I didn't want to burst into tears and cause a scene.

That was the last time I saw Julius in the house. That day marked the last kiss on his cheek I gave him before he went into the hospital. It took me two years before I allowed myself to grieve the loss of one of the greatest loves of my life. Still, that moment between us is still clear more than twenty-five years later.

I am thankful for the safe foundation he laid for me in my formative years. My experiences with my family helped shape who I have become today. While my parents' and grandparents' influence helped me along my life's journey, I had to figure out my truths about myself and life.

My First Love

In 2003, Rick flew out to Scottsdale, Arizona, with me on a business trip. It was our first trip together. He intended to propose to me. The proposal was romantic and unexpected. I cried a very ugly cry once I realized what he was doing. I felt lucky to have found such a gentleman after having no real dating experience at that point. My granddaddy Julius would have loved Rick as my other grandparents and parents did.

At age twenty-six, I landed a new job, received my bachelor's degree, and became Mrs. Flanagan. Life was pretty good. For the majority of our marriage, Rick and I shared a beautiful relationship. It seemed like one of the biggest challenges in our relationship was the impact of outside influences, whether from people's expectations or situations beyond our control. They added pressure and sometimes pulled our attention away from each other and what we were trying to build. Those external dynamics formed later in our marriage created tension, making it difficult for us to stay grounded in our connections. Prior to that we had a really good thing going for a long time. We found lots of ways to be adventurous and have fun together. We're both pretty romantic.

There were times throughout our marriage when I thought Rick was God's gift to me. His love was proof that I was lovable and wanted. For most of our marriage, I cared more about his happiness than my own.

Rick has a son from his first marriage. I was nervous and overly cautious about being a stepmom to Rick's son. It was important to me that his son felt loved, too, and a part of us. Before our marriage, we went to counseling together. I read books on becoming a blended family and listened to tapes on the topic on my way to and from work. I would discuss what I was learning with Rick.

Throughout our marriage, I tended to push myself to get more out of life, always reaching and exploring different concepts. The status quo never worked for me. Getting lost in books and stories is an all-time favorite pastime of mine. Bookstores are still one of my favorite places to go.

There have been so many teachers and countless people who have touched my life and helped fan the flames that were burning inside me. Movies and documentaries made me want to explore life more. People and life intrigue me. I'm fascinated by it all and want to experience the fullness of it. I used to be ashamed of being oriented this way because not many people around me shared my excitement to learn more, at least not in the way I did.

My dear husband was more comfortable with life as it is, which was not wrong of him. Rick had ambition and loved to travel, but he wasn't interested in exploring the depth of love and relationships like I was. Around year fifteen of our marriage, we both realized that we wanted different things out of life.

At the time, I couldn't explain how we both started moving apart. During that period, I was definitely trying to figure myself out. Rick was the person I wanted to talk to about everything so that he could help me sort things out. He was my best friend, and I trusted him. But I came to realize that I couldn't share everything.

Rick loved the comfort and opportunities that came with my salary, but I was burnt out. I had a bad experience at a company that recruited me. It turned out to be a toxic environment that took a lot out of me and my marriage.

By this time, it seemed our paths were widening in different directions. I couldn't understand it at first. Some of the personal interests we once shared were gone. I think some of it had to do with the influences of new friendships and the dynamic of a family member that brought different values, ones that didn't support the kind of connection we built and were trying to maintain. This reflection isn't to place blame on anyone, but it affected the closeness we once had. It became hard to figure out how to make our union work.

I gave our marriage everything I could, but I still felt like I broke us. I didn't know how to stuff myself back into a shape that made it comfortable for both of us. I took responsibility for our entire marriage falling apart, which I now know was unhealthy on my part.

Rick's death almost took me out. I've wanted to give up more times than I'd like to admit. I was no longer afraid of dying. During the deepest part of my grief, I recalled these words from bell hooks, "We can never go back. I know that now. We can go forward . . . When the mourning ceased, I was able to love again."[3] I was hoping hooks was right about the last part, that one day I would feel love again, period, not necessarily romantic love, just love.

Today, I'm a full-time relationship intelligence coach with a specific focus on clarity, self-awareness, meaningful connections, and emotional intelligence. Being this type of coach while living life in real time is no small feat. It's actually downright hard at times because my personal life has its ups and downs like everyone else.

I still have work to do as well. If you could hear my inner thoughts at times, you'd hear me repeatedly saying, "Keep your heart soft and open, Charmaine, You've got this. Love is here."

I have to remind myself of this because, for a long time, my default mechanism was to shut my emotions off so I didn't feel pain so much. But what gets pushed down eventually bubbles to the surface over and over again until it's dealt with. It has been the most beautiful, terrifying, heartbreaking, yet life-giving ride of my life.

> For a long time, my default mechanism was to shut my emotions off so I didn't feel pain so much. But what gets pushed down eventually bubbles to the surface over and over again until it's dealt with.

What To Expect From This Book

Let your teacher be love itself.
—RUMI

As coined by the host of the podcast *At Home With Byron Katie*, we are in Earth school.[4] In this Earth school experience, all of life's experiences, if you let them, are here to teach us.

We all have our own unique paths in this life. I don't believe there is only one blueprint to getting through life. This book is written to offer some guidance as you navigate through the barriers that may be holding you back from the love you desire.

This book is not just a collection of words—I've taken great consideration in what I'm sharing because for far too long I think love has been mishandled by all of us. Within these pages, I will share some of the tools I've used to help me rise to a greater level of love. I share a bit of my personal story to help you understand where I'm coming from. There is no way around it. I had to get comfortable with sharing more about myself because I am a private person.

Here's what I tell my clients and now you, my dear reader: Keep what feels right and release what doesn't. Consider all things and be open to possibilities. Allow your inner wisdom to be your guide as I share what I've learned with you.

Your Opportunity: LoveWork Homework

At the end of each chapter, you will find words of encouragement. You will also have a chance to reflect and do "LoveWork" (homework) on your own. You will have the opportunity to identify and work on dismantling the barriers on your path that hinder you from experiencing the life you want to experience. I encourage you to use these tools as more than just good exercises.

We are not going after perfection here because there is no such thing. But consistent practice using the tools provided can create ease and flow in life.

If you need support at any point in this book, please contact a trusted therapist, counselor, or credentialed coach who is well-versed in this work.

Defining Love

Many times, when I talk about love, people think I'm chasing rainbows and unicorns, which is far from the truth. Love is not arbitrary to me: it's sacred and precious. For far too long, we've mishandled love and abused its name. It's time to give it due respect and serious consideration.

A few years back, if you were to ask me to define love, I would have given you a definition and even quoted some of my teachers' definitions of love. Today, I find that trying to define love is like boxing in the vastness of the entire universe.

What I've come to understand is that love is felt through words and actions. The experience of real love is undeniable.

This is not a definition, but a nod to you trusting yourself when it comes to your experience of love and how you feel. You know when love is present and when it isn't. Becoming more aware is where we will begin.

Love springs from awareness.
—Anthony De Mello

Awareness

The key is to sharpen your self-awareness skills. You can do this by practicing mindfulness: staying present in the moment, noticing things as they happen, and observing what's going on inside of you.

Self-awareness is your North Star. As you read this book, paying close attention to your thoughts, emotions, and behaviors will help you. Check in with your feelings as well; however, don't get overly identified with your feelings. If you need support, please contact a professional.

Whoever said love is blind is dead wrong.
Love is the only thing that lets us see each other
with the remotest accuracy.
—MARTHA BECK

May this book help you see love and experience love more clearly and accurately.

Chapter 1

Barrier:
Holding On To The Past

"I See Thoughts"
by Toni Jones, Affirmation Musician &
Mental Health Spiritualist

I release the drama of others from my past and I joyfully create more conscious connections. But I study me before I judge and create a story about others. Thank you everybody for being exactly what my growth needed to be for me.

*I*t was a beautiful Saturday morning in the spring of 2011. Rick had plans so I used that time to meditate and journal. I sat comfortably on the floor of my office with my back leaning against the chaise lounge chair. With my eyes closed, I attempted to meditate.

Those of you who practice meditation know how challenging it can be at times. My thoughts went to my childhood. Instead of focusing back on my breath, I allowed those thoughts to play out. I was thinking about how I was treated by certain family members and friends. I was recounting incidents that hurt me. I felt myself get upset and then sad.

Before that morning, I was aware that I was holding on to some things in the past, but I was not aware of how it was still affecting me. After some time, I went back to my breath.

Once my meditation was over, I grabbed my notebook and pen, climbed on the chaise, and began writing. My writing was about all the grievances I had from my childhood. I wrote until I got all of it out. Over several weeks, I went back to that journal writing—this time with the intention of letting go of it all.

Over those couple of weeks, I realized it was interfering with my current life. I was reacting to current life situations based on past experiences. I was reliving the past over and over again. I was overly identified with the past, not fully living in the present.

Here's where things got interesting for me. After several journal entries, I realized I was blaming people from my past for why I couldn't live my life the way I wanted to. They were responsible for why I couldn't fully be happy and free.

I couldn't believe I was unconsciously living with that belief, but it was true. In many ways, I was that young girl who was hurt. This was an uncomfortable realization.

All that time, I was holding myself and the people from my past hostage in my mind. I carried them and the situation into my present life, unwillingly on their part, I'm sure. Most of them I was no longer connected to in any real way. I'm sure none of them had a clue that I was holding on to what happened between us.

It didn't make sense the more I thought about it. It was time to release us. So what if they never apologize? What if they could never make it "right" by me? What if they saw what happened differently? What if they weren't sorry? What if I was the one who was wrong?

I needed to take responsibility for my life, my happiness, and my well-being. Working on the barrier of holding on to the past also showed me that I was retraumatizing myself over and over again. Physician and author Gabor Maté said, "Trauma is not what happens to you, it's what happens inside you as a result of what happened to you."[5] Exploring what happened inside me was the key, and it set me free. What I saw was that I had developed low self-esteem, trust issues, hypervigilance, and more.

For those of you working through past trauma, especially from your childhood, we instinctively blame ourselves when something bad happens. In the book, *What Happened to You? Conversation on Trauma, Resilience, and Healing*, authors Bruce D. Perry and Oprah Winfrey share that, "Children are not born bad. They are shaped by what happens to them. A child exposed to chaos, neglect, or violence is not responsible for what those experiences do to their developing brain."[6] Children don't have the knowledge or power to prevent or protect those things from happening to them. The adults, however, are responsible for the child's well-being.

In the book, *The Body Keeps the Score*, Dr. Bessel van der Kolk said, "The parent-child connection is the most powerful mental health intervention known to mankind."[7] It is through the lens of our caregivers that we understand life and relationships.

Healing childhood trauma is possible with the help of a professional who specializes in trauma recovery. The good news is that, as an adult, you can now reclaim your power and take back control of your life. You can now give yourself the grace to have a say in the matter of how life will go from here on out.

Understanding Holding On To The Past

Holding on to the past can feel like carrying a heavy weight on your shoulders. When you keep clinging to old wounds, regrets, or mistakes, it keeps you stuck in a loop, reliving the pain over and over again. The hurt from the past keeps haunting you, and instead of living fully in the present, you're trapped in yesterday's shadows.

> Holding on to the past can feel like carrying a heavy weight on your shoulders. When you keep clinging to old wounds, regrets, or mistakes, it keeps you stuck in a loop, reliving the pain over and over again. The hurt from the past keeps haunting you . . ..

This can drown you in emotions like anger, shame, and sadness, making it harder to move forward and embrace what's happening in the present moment. We tend to miss a lot in our lives. It becomes a wall between you and the life you want, blocking your growth and stealing your peace. You may hold back from new experiences or connections because you're afraid of being hurt again, never fully letting yourself live or feel joy.

The longer you hold on, the harder it becomes to heal. Letting go isn't easy, but it's the key to freeing yourself from that burden, so you can finally breathe, start fresh, and open yourself to the possibilities of the future.

Author Gary Zukav said, "Your life is yours to live, no matter how you choose to live it. When you do not think about how you intend to live it, it lives you. When you occupy it, step into it consciously, you live it."[8]

I needed to take responsibility for how I show up in life now. I am responsible for the choices I make now.

Responsibility felt burdensome when I first tried to take responsibility for my life. So, I took some time to research responsibility and found this quote online by Werner Erhard, an American lecturer, that made sense to me. The latter part of Erhard's explanation on responsibility helped clear things up for me. He shared, "Being responsible starts with the willingness to deal with a situation from the view of life that you are the generator of what you do, what you have, and what you are. That is not the truth. It is a place to stand. No one can make you responsible, nor can you impose responsibility on another. It is a grace you give yourself—an empowering context that leaves you with a say in the matter of life."[9]

I can't go back and change the past. I can choose to heal, to let go, and free myself and everyone else who was directly or indirectly affected.

Slowly and gently letting go of the blame, shame, and judgment, I started to soften. This is where I began to understand what genuine compassion, grace, and forgiveness truly meant.

We are all trying to figure it out. With time, I no longer wanted to hold anyone to the past.

Unhealthy Patterns Of Behavior When Holding On To The Past

The past hurts; the words unspoken, the wounds unhealed, and the moments we never fully processed don't just stay in the past. They shape how we show up today. And more often than not, we're unaware of just how deeply they're influencing our daily interactions.

They affect the stories we tell ourselves. The love we think we deserve. The boundaries we're afraid to set. And the patterns we keep repeating even when they no longer serve us.

Unhealed pain doesn't just disappear. It seeps into our relationships, our reactions, and the parts of us that still believe we need to stay guarded to stay safe.

With grace and compassion for ourselves, we can begin to gently explore the unhealthy patterns that formed from the pain of our past not to blame, shame or judge ourselves, but to free ourselves.

Here's the research I found on unhealthy patterns that emerge when we continue to hold onto past hurts.

We Become Emotionally Unavailable Or Emotionally Guarded

One of the most common responses to being hurt is creating protective barriers to shield us from any potential emotional hurt or vulnerability. After being hurt by someone we trusted, the idea of letting someone in again feels too risky and dangerous. As a result, we may create an emotional fortress, guarding ourselves from vulnerability.

While this self-protection may initially feel safe, it also prevents us from forming deep, meaningful connections.

We Become Emotionally Detached

Some people carefully control their emotions by guarding them. Others become emotionally detached by disconnecting from their emotions altogether as a way of coping and as a means of self-protection.

Emotional detachment isolates us from the love, intimacy, and support we desire and deserve.

We Develop Trust Issues

Trust is foundational to any relationship. When trust is broken, especially by someone close to us, it can shatter us and cast doubt on all other relationships. We may begin to question the intentions of others, assume the worst, or expect to be betrayed or rejected. We can also become hypervigilant, which can be exhausting.

We Become People Pleasers

People-pleasing stems from our fear of rejection or abandonment. We believe if we keep others happy, they won't leave us. We want to avoid the pain of losing them. We often neglect our own needs, wants, and desires by prioritizing the care of others.

This people-pleasing tendency is draining and leaves us feeling empty.

We Become Conflict Avoidant

For some of us, past hurt creates a deep aversion to conflict. If past disagreements or confrontations led to rejection or emotional pain, we may try to avoid difficult conversations at all costs. We suppress our emotions, hide our needs, or settle for less than we deserve.

Avoiding conflict might seem easier in the short term, but it often creates resentment. It makes it difficult to bond with others.

We Self-Blame Or Feel Guilty

There's a tendency to blame ourselves or feel guilty, even when we're not responsible for the actions of others. The pain is internalized, and somehow we believe we caused the hurt.

This can damage our self-worth. Our self-worth is not determined by the hurt others inflict on us.

> Our self-worth is not determined by the hurt others inflict on us.

We Fear Rejection Or Abandonment

The fear of being rejected or abandoned again can be overwhelming once you've been deeply hurt. We might become overly cautious, avoid intimacy, or even push others away before they can hurt us.

We Become Cautious With Our Communication

When we've been hurt, it feels safer to shut down or avoid sharing our true feelings. Withholding vulnerability or only sharing surface-level thoughts often stems from the fear of being misunderstood or judged.

This pattern creates distance in relationships.

We Become Perfectionistic

Perfectionism can serve as a way to shield ourselves from past pain by constructing an illusion of control. It is the fear of criticism, failure, or rejection that drives this behavior. If we can make everything perfect— our actions, how we look, and how we perform—then we might feel like nothing can go wrong.

This does a number on our self-worth because there tends to be a persistent feeling of never measuring up.

We Emotionally Numb Out

Some people, when faced with intense emotional pain, turn to numbing behaviors. Numbing behaviors are things like substance abuse, overeating or undereating, workaholism, or gaming.

Emotional numbing keeps us from fully experiencing or processing our feelings. While it might provide temporary relief, it also prevents healing and can deepen the emotional wounds we're trying to avoid.

We Become Cynical

After being hurt, it can be tempting to adopt a cynical outlook on life. With cynicism, there's a belief that people are inherently selfish, that love is a myth, or that nothing good will ever come our way. Some people even become apathetic toward relationships or life, in general, as a defense mechanism against future disappointment.

We Avoid Intimacy

Emotional and physical intimacy can feel unsafe after being hurt. We might avoid getting too close to others, resisting vulnerability, or pushing away people who try to get close. This avoidance comes from the belief that intimacy equals potential pain, and that keeping our distance will shield us from future hurt, but that can be just as painful.

We Tend To Overthink Or Become Hypervigilant

Some of us form a habit of overthinking or becoming hypervigilant after being hurt over and over again. It's because our brain is trying to process the pain and make sense of what happened in order to regain safety.

It also leads to a lot of rumination because we're trying to understand what happened, get closure, or find a way to prevent it from happening again.

Practicing New Healthy Patterns When Releasing Past Hurts

Healing from past hurts is a deeply personal journey—one that requires more than simply moving on. Now that we've identified some unhealthy patterns we've developed in response to pain, we can practice healthier ways of behaving and relating that foster emotional resilience and personal growth. As we release the grip of old wounds, we begin to reclaim our power, creating space for a more fulfilling and authentic life.

Allow Yourself To Let Your Guard Down A Little At A Time

Practice with others by allowing yourself to be emotionally present with a trusted person or two. Surround yourself with safe people. Take your time and practice being emotionally available with them. Take one small step at a time.

Gaining a greater understanding of your emotions can help you figure out if what you are feeling stems from past experiences, and if so, how to get present with what's happening now. Psychologist Susan David shares that, "emotions are data, they are not directives."[10] Our emotions are valuable information, but not necessarily something you should automatically react to.

Consider Rebuilding Trust

Where can you go when trust has been broken? Rebuilding trust takes time, patience, discernment, and effort. Learning to trust yourself is the most important step when you are redirecting the unhealthy pattern of mistrust in a healthy direction. It takes the willingness, emotional maturity, and effort to see it through. Take some time to reflect on what happened. If you are having trouble understanding what happened, get support from a trusted therapist or coach.

Practice Authenticity And Self-Respect

Honoring your inner truth is living authentically. Aligning with your values and feelings, rather than trying to conform to external expectations of others, is living with integrity. There is no need for self-abandonment in hopes that it will keep others in your life. Being more self-aware and accepting yourself is key.

Constantly seeking approval from others will leave you depleted and exhausted. The way you view yourself matters more than anyone else's thoughts or opinions of you.

Practice Healthy Approaches To Conflict

There is no way around it, conflict will happen. You will not always agree with others. Expressing our differences in opinion or otherwise in a healthy manner is the goal. It's the willingness to stay healthy with each other even when conflict happens. Emotional intelligence is important. There are healthy approaches to conflict.

Healthy conflict is necessary for growth and understanding in relationships. It can lead to stronger, more resilient bonds. When conflict arises, we want to avoid judgment, blame, shaming, or criticism.

Slow Your Thoughts Down

Overthinking or hypervigilance is a response to feeling unsafe. If we let them, our thoughts can create quite a story. Checking in with yourself is an important step. It helps you regain control over your emotional well-being. Building a trusting relationship with yourself is key. Above all else, trust yourself.

Take notice of your thoughts. Are you imagining worst-case scenarios? Often, overthinking involves playing out irrational fears. Ask yourself if the situation you're imagining is likely to happen.

Simply asking for clarity is so helpful. Talking it over with the person involved in the hurt can clear up some of the confusion. If you can't talk to the person or people involved, a trusted professional or friend can give you a fresh perspective.

Build Your Self-Worth Muscle

Committing to honoring our humanity with compassion and care is important when we are working on our self-worth. It requires us to create a renewed relationship with ourselves, changing the way we speak to ourselves and others.

Be mindful of the company you keep. The people you interact with can have a big impact on your sense of self-worth. Surround yourself with those who uplift you, support your growth, and encourage you to be the best version of yourself. You will do yourself a big favor by avoiding toxic relationships that drain your energy or make you feel inferior. Create distance and set boundaries with people who don't treat you with respect and kindness. No one has the right to determine your worth: only you do.

One quick way to lower your self-worth is to compare yourself to others. Singer, songwriter, and actress Jill Scott shared her wisdom during an interview where she was asked if she is nervous about performing after Erykah Badu. Her response: "We all have our own thing, that's the magic. Everybody comes with their own sense of strength and their own sense of queendom. Mine could never compare to hers, and hers could never compare to mine."[11]

Everyone has their own path, and we all grow and develop at different rates. Instead of measuring yourself against others, focus on your own progress and journey. When you catch yourself comparing, remind yourself that everyone's life is unique, including yours. Celebrate your own magic.

Know That You Are OK Even When The Answer Is No

Dealing with rejection or abandonment is painful. We have all had to face rejection or abandonment at some point in our lives; it hurts.

It became apparent that I needed to work on my unhealthy pattern of staying too long in relationships that aren't healthy for me for fear of rejection and abandonment.

"If someone tells you 'no' or rejects you, that's good news; it's pointing us to the right place. We don't want to be anywhere where the answer is 'no.' We want to be where the answer is 'yes,'" author Byron Katie wisely shared during one of her podcasts.[12]

Practice Open Communication

Practicing open communication after being hurt involves giving yourself time to process your emotions before expressing them honestly. Use "I" statements to share how you feel without blaming the other person, and focus on your needs for healing. Stay calm, listen to the other person's perspective, and set boundaries if necessary.

Avoid attacking or accusing, and instead, focus on your feelings and the impact of the situation. Vulnerability is key, so be open to forgiveness and growth, even if the conversation is difficult.

By being honest and clear, you pave the way for understanding and healing in the relationship.

Practice Intimacy

Practicing intimacy after being hurt in the past can feel daunting, but it's also an opportunity to heal and connect in a deeper way. It begins with acknowledging your pain without letting it control your future. Take your time—there's no rush. Let yourself be vulnerable in small, manageable ways, and gently share your fears, your scars, and your hopes.

Communication is essential, not just for expressing your needs, but also for understanding the other person's heart. Deepening intimacy is something that's built little by little, so be patient with yourself and with the process.

Healing and intimacy can coexist, but it takes courage to open up again, to trust that you deserve love and closeness. It's about embracing vulnerability, slowly rebuilding trust, and letting yourself feel safe enough to truly connect once more.

Honor Your Humanity

Do you struggle with perfectionism? Are you harder on yourself than you need to be? Do you sell yourself short in many cases? Does the "I'm not good enough" statement run through your mind over and over again? Throughout my life, I noticed the women in my life struggled with this far more than men do. After doing some research, I found article after article written to confirm what I was noticing and experiencing.

Here are some ways I've addressed my own desire to be perfect. It started with my accepting that I am simply a wonderful being. Many of us are taught that we are flawed and need fixing. Yet, if we take the time to see, truly see, who we are, we will see that we are having a human experience here; that's it. Accepting our humanity is important.

Author Gregg Braden shared in his book, *The Divine Matrix*, "In our beliefs about who we are, what we have and don't have, and what should and shouldn't be, we breathe life into our greatest joys as well as our darkest moments."[13] Taking the time to check in with what we truly believe about ourselves, we can begin to change any belief that contradicts the truth of who we are.

We have all experienced setbacks, disappointments, and pain, and we're still here. You're here reading this book right now. You picked yourself up, again; please keep going.

We all have made mistakes. The gift is when we allow ourselves to learn from them and keep moving forward. When we learn the lesson and apply it to our lives, it lightens the hold perfectionism has on us. It's also a way of loving yourself.

Stay Connected To Emotions

Staying connected to your emotions, without overly identifying with them, is important. After being hurt in the past, this is a delicate and brave act of self-care.

It's about allowing yourself to truly feel what's inside—whether it's the lingering sadness, the sharpness of anger, or the weight of fear—without running from it. You don't have to push these feelings away or hide them, because they're a part of you, and you deserve to honor them.

Give yourself the grace to feel fully, even if it feels uncomfortable or overwhelming. Create space for your emotions—through writing, talking with someone you trust, or simply sitting in quiet reflection. Let your heart speak, even if it's hard, because every emotion you allow yourself to experience is a step toward healing.

By staying connected to your true feelings, you give yourself the chance to heal, grow, and reclaim your sense of wholeness, one feeling at a time.

Look For The Good

Experiencing any form of trauma or abuse is never good for us. Looking for the good in past hurtful experiences isn't about pretending the pain didn't happen or excusing the actions of others—it's about reclaiming your power and finding meaning in the healing process. When we reflect on how we've grown or the inner strength we've discovered through adversity, we shift from being defined by our wounds to being shaped by our resilience. This shift can help us break harmful patterns, cultivate deeper empathy, and begin to see ourselves not as victims of our past but as survivors who are actively choosing a healthier, more empowered future. Finding the good doesn't erase the hurt, but it transforms the story we carry forward.

Now that we've addressed both unhealthy and healthy patterns of behavior we have formed, we are going to address our past and others.

Our Past And Others

The health of a community depends on the health of the individuals within that community. If we all chose to take care of ourselves so that we could support each other we would create a healthier environment, giving us the ability to thrive. Healing from the past is a gift to not just yourself but your community.

Loving others well also allows them the dignity and respect for their own path, their own choices. I used to think I knew what was best for others but that was not true. I could offer a perspective, but I don't know best.

Sometimes the path will take different turns from where you expected but it turns out OK in the end.

We are only responsible for the choices we make and for our own well-being. Nonadult children, elderly parents or adults with disabilities, and pets are excluded from what I'm talking about of course. I am talking about able-bodied, sound adults.

To our own detriment, we've all formed unhealthy behaviors where one person is overly responsible while the other person takes hardly any responsibility. This behavior from both sides damages relationships. It can wreak havoc on our physical and mental well-being.

We all have the ability to rise to the occasion. I've seen it happen over and over again. When we balance the responsibility scale, people really do rise or they go off and find someone else who will keep them in the cycle of unhealthy behaviors, which is one of the ways toxic bonds form.

Letting go of being responsible for others can be a hard thing to do, especially in a relationship where two people are used to the dance of "you take care of me and I let you." When either party decides to switch up the dance moves, watch out. The person who is used to the normal dance will fight for things to go back to the way they were.

It's essential to establish boundaries when deciding to return responsibility to the person it belongs to. I have a chapter dedicated to boundaries.

We are each other's keepers. We can care for, support, and even offer guidance in certain situations, but we are not entirely responsible for others. We are actually hurting someone and cutting them off from personal growth when we take away their ability to act, make decisions, or take charge of their emotional well-being.

Each person is responsible for their own choices, feelings, and actions. If you can allow that, the role you desire in the lives of those you love expands significantly. Your love is sufficient.

Encouragement

Healing from past experiences is where our personal power lies. Taking responsibility for how we show up for ourselves and with others now allows for real connection to happen.

Changing patterns of behavior is challenging. I see why many decide not to take on personal growth: It's hard work. Looking at our "stuff" is not easy. Life can take a sharp turn at times, and the rug will feel like it's been pulled from underneath you. During this healing journey, some may walk away from you. You may think you can't do this, but you absolutely can.

Keep moving forward. People may leave you, but don't ever leave yourself. You will gain meaningful, nourishing relationships that far exceed what you had before. There are people who will stay with you. You've got this.

Whenever I look back at young Charmaine and all the suffering she held on to, I send myself extra love and compassion. We are all doing the best we can. Like author Dr. Maya Angelou said, "Do the best you can until you know better. Then, when you know better, do better."[14]

LoveWork—Your Opportunity

Are there any grievances you are still holding onto from the past? If so, please write them below or use your personal journal to write them out one grievance at a time.

_____

_____

_____

_____

Do you want to release the pain of the past? If so, what new patterns of behavior will you practice to help you heal? (If you need support, please reach out to a trusted therapist, counselor, or credentialed coach to help you.)

_____

_____

_____

_____

Bonus

An Intention Agreement for A More Meaningful Life

I, _____, intend to give myself the grace to have a say in the matter of my life from this day forward. I intend to live an empowering life. I will no longer put myself through unnecessary suffering. I will take excellent care of myself, mind, body, and spirit. I will seek the help of a licensed therapist, certified coach, or counselor if I need support. I am committed to creating a more meaningful life for myself.

Please write any additional intentions you would like to make to yourself:

_____

_____

_____

_____

_____

_____

_____

_____

Chapter 2

Barrier:
Lack Of Self-Care

I have come to believe that caring for myself is not self-indulgent.
Caring for myself is an act of survival.
—AUDRE LORDE

Dduring an interview, I was asked to define self-care. Here's how I define self-care:

> To deeply nourish oneself. It requires intimacy, attention, and an inherent sense of self-worth. Self-care is to be in tune with yourself. It is about knowing, respecting, and honoring your feelings, needs, wants, and desires. It's knowing when boundaries are necessary. It's tending to your mental and physical health. It's a way of life.

Remember how you behaved when you felt like you had found that special someone? You unleashed the wooer in you, didn't you? You put your best foot forward. You paid close attention to what they needed, wanted, and desired. You wanted to know everything about them. You showed great care for that person. If your beloved sneezed, you ran for the tissues. You would even think ahead of all of the ways you could show how much you cared.

While the goal was to win their affection, you also wanted the person to know how important they were to you.

Have you ever considered what it would be like to give yourself that level of care?

As I worked on my self-care practice, I used it as a barometer for how much love I had for myself. It was through the acts of care and the lack of it that I could see where I placed my love for myself. The same was true for those in my life.

Recognition Of The Barrier

Did I take basic care of myself? Yes, I showered daily, never missed a dentist appointment, got massages, and went for hikes, among other things.

Nevertheless, was I nurturing my well-being? Not to the best of my ability. I was so busy trying to check the boxes of being successful in life: being a good wife, a good coworker, a good friend, and a mentor. I was caring for everyone else's wants, needs, and desires, and I constantly neglected my own. There was no one to blame. It was the beliefs underneath that behavior that I later discovered were why I was showing up in life like that.

One of the beliefs I had was that good people take care of others first; it is selfish to put myself first.

Another belief was that if I cared about others and put their needs first, they wouldn't leave. I'm not quite sure when that belief was formed. Admitting that belief hurt because I feared that I would never be enough, and others would eventually leave me.

Because of those two beliefs, I gave away all my care.

I was constantly exhausted taking care of everyone else, even when they didn't need me to. I trained those closest to me that I would care for them first and always. No wonder I developed high blood pressure.

In every aspect of my life, I gave myself away. I put my all into work, family, friendships, volunteering, you name it. I am a hard worker, but to my own demise. If I wanted to get better, I needed to practice self-care. It became essential to my well-being.

Understanding Self-Care

Author of the book *The Body Is Not An Apology; The Power of Radical Self-Love*, Sonya Renee Taylor says, "To build a world that works for everyone, we must first make the radical decision to love every facet of ourselves."[15]

Tricia Hersey, author of *Rest Is Resistance: A Manifesto*, shares this: "I want us to understand that nuance is freeing and freedom. There is no such thing as cookie-cutter healing. Everyone brings with them an origin story, a history, and interconnected identities. There is room to rest in the freedom of managing your own deprogramming journey. It is never either/or and always both/and. You don't have to grind, hustle, accept burnout as normal, and be in a constant state of exhaustion and sleep deprivation. You don't have to kill yourself spiritually or physically to live a fruitful life."[16]

The way I began this journey of care was by committing to treating myself the way I believe my greatest lover and friend would. I went back to the drawing board. I thought about how I offered care to the people I loved. Specifically, I considered how I cared for Rick, how much I cared about his well-being. I decided to practice that for myself as well.

It was uncomfortable. I was even embarrassed at first. I also felt like I shouldn't be this audacious. I was mindful of not neglecting Rick or anyone else as I practiced care for myself. It was an adjustment for everyone and not always well-received.

I had to get used to disappointing others because I no longer wanted to continue to disappoint myself. My greatest lover and friend wouldn't want that for me.

> The way I began this journey of care was by committing to treating myself the way I believe my greatest lover and friend would.

Unhealthy Patterns Of Behavior Developed With The Lack Of Self-Care

Here's what I learned when I studied the unhealthy patterns of the lack of self-care.

We Lack Boundaries

We have a hard time with boundaries on both sides. We don't know how to set them for ourselves, and we cross the boundaries of others. There are times when we overcommit, trying to be all things to all people. For those of us who are used to being everyone's caregiver, we have a hard time allowing others to take care of themselves. We are convinced that without us they won't survive.

We Prioritize Others

Some of us fall into the pattern of neglecting ourselves to take care of everyone else. We don't even think about ourselves or feel we can think about ourselves until everyone else is cared for. Oftentimes we suppress our needs and emotions.

We Feel Taken Advantage Of

It's our own doing, but we can do things like overcommit, overgive, and people-please, and then feel taken advantage of. Our self-worth and value are off, so we can find ourselves in this predicament. We can start to resent people when we overgive and people-please.

We Become Physically Exhausted

Have you ever felt tired, even after a full night's sleep? That was me all the time. It was my life for years. Here in America, we tend to overexert ourselves, not eat well, and not exercise properly. We don't give ourselves time to recover before we are off to the next thing.

I attended an event where the speaker did a lot of yelling at the audience to stop resting. He said, "Sleep when you are dead." There are still parts of our society that shame others for prioritizing rest. In the Black community, especially, we are considered lazy if we aren't grinding constantly. This abuse from our oppressors has been passed down through generations. Author Tricia Hersey's explanation of how we've come to be like this is in her book *Rest Is Resistance: A Manifesto*. Hersey shares, "We are socialized into systems that cause us to conform and believe our worth is connected to how much we can produce. Our constant labor becomes a prison that allows us to be disembodied. We become easy for the systems to manipulate, disconnected from our power as divine beings, and hopeless. We forget how to dream. This is how grind culture continues. We internalize the lies and in turn become agents of an unsustainable way of living."

In addition, she also acknowledges the unique experience of black women and women of color when it comes to labor. "I feel like a legacy of exhaustion resides somewhere in all of us, but specifically resides in the bodies of those who have melanated skin."

We Experience Mental Burnout

We are in a fast-paced, ever-changing world. We are constantly being fed information. Our phone alone is a source of constant information. It can be challenging to fully turn off for fear of missing out.

We are more stressed than ever because our brains don't get the proper rest or recovery period.

We Experience Emotional Exhaustion

While acute stress is a part of life, it seems like chronic stress has taken the helm of our lives. Anxiety is on the rise. Whether we are dealing with our own emotions, the emotions of those we live with, or work dynamics, it can leave us exhausted.

We Self-Isolate

When things get tough, some of us close the world off instead of getting help or support. We start to neglect the important relationships in our lives.

We Develop Physical Symptoms

Neglecting self-care can lead to headaches and even migraines, muscle tension, backaches, and more.

We Develop Eating Disorders

When we aren't caring for ourselves emotionally or understanding our own needs, we can develop eating habits that are harmful to our well-being. Eating disorders are a symptom of the lack of self-care.

Practicing New Patterns Of Self-Care

To counter the old unhealthy patterns, I had to practice new behaviors. Here are some new practices I took on—and you can too.

Prioritize Yourself

Taking care of yourself will also allow you the space to support your loved ones and friends, but from a more generative place. Below is a passage from the book *Calling in "The One."* I use it as a reminder of the way I need to care for myself. Author Katherine Woodward Thomas—my mentor and teacher—shares an example of a letter someone could write to their beloved-to-be. This letter is self-care.

> My Beloved, I will always have the courage to be honest with you. To guard your heart and protect the integrity of our love by telling you the truth. I am also willing to hear your truth and invite you to be completely honest with me as the foundation of our love.
>
> Beloved, I welcome your true feelings and needs and I promise to do my best to accommodate them whenever possible. Rest assured that your feelings and needs matter to me, and I am grateful to be the guardian of your heart. Beloved, I'm happy when you take care of yourself first and foremost! I honor your boundaries and support you to do everything you know to do to take excellent care of your heart, soul, body, and mind.[17]

I rewrote the letter, inserting my own name where you see "Beloved." I hope to share this kind of care and love with my future beloved. Until then, I am offering this to myself as an act of radical self-care.

Set Healthy Boundaries

Setting boundaries is a new pattern that took me a long time to establish, and I'll keep it brief here since I've dedicated an entire chapter later to it.

Here's how I approached it: First, check in with yourself by paying attention to your feelings and needs—ask yourself if you feel safe, respected, and valued, and recognize your limitations. Honor your boundaries when you don't feel those things, remembering that you're also working on your self-worth.

Next, be clear with others by expressing what works for you and what doesn't. Letting others know your boundaries and the consequences of crossing them is a healthy way of relating. As Dr. Brené Brown wisely says, "Clear is kind; unclear is unkind."[18] It's equally important to respect others' boundaries, as everyone deserves to feel safe.

Lastly, stay firm. When you start changing your patterns, others may resist, get upset, or speak negatively. If you're a recovering people pleaser, those who are used to you accommodating them may react strongly, but it's essential to hold firm to your boundaries.

> Be clear with others by expressing what works for you and what doesn't. Letting others know your boundaries and the consequences of crossing them is a healthy way of relating.

Make Room To Enjoy The New You

This is your chance to stop overcommitting and overgiving to others and instead focus on doing things that bring you joy. Remember, caring for yourself is like loving your greatest friend or partner—you deserve that time and attention.

Your loved ones likely want more of your presence, to enjoy your company. However, take time to play and engage in activities you love, even if it's been a while since you did. Allow yourself to daydream—find your favorite spot, lay back, and let your mind wander freely.

Also, consider taking yourself on a date, which can be incredibly enjoyable. I started doing this even when I was married, and I recall my husband appreciating that I took time for myself outside of our shared time together. I learned this practice from Julia Cameron's *The Artist's Way*, where she encourages people to take "artist dates."[19] She suggests setting aside time each week to nurture your creative self, without any obligations or judgment, and to explore your own interests and curiosities. The best part is, it doesn't always have to cost money.

Rest

I haven't found anyone who talks about rest as powerfully as author Tricia Hersey; she is truly the expert on the subject. It's because of her that I've come to understand and honor the sacredness of rest. In her book, *Rest Is Resistance: A Manifesto*, she writes, "Treating each other and ourselves with care isn't a luxury, but an absolute necessity if we're going to thrive. Resting isn't an afterthought, but a basic part of being human."[20]

This really resonates with me, especially when considering how vital rest is for our well-being. Going to bed on time is crucial, and how we prepare for sleep plays a significant role. Consider turning your bedtime routine into a calming ritual, almost like a sweet lullaby.

Napping is also an underrated way to restore energy—if you can, take naps, even if just for a short time, as they can give you the boost you need to get through the day. On your days off, try to make naps a regular part of your routine.

Finally, stepping away from social media and the news is essential for maintaining mental health. These outlets can increase stress and anxiety, so taking breaks from them provides the space to do things you enjoy, ultimately supporting your overall well-being.

Get Support

If you are feeling emotionally, physically, and mentally exhausted, there are several outlets to help you: inspirational music, podcasts, books, TED talks, and thought leaders on YouTube. A trusted therapist, counselor, or credentialed coach can help you if the practice of self-care challenges you.

Engage With Your Community

Sometimes, good company is all you need. Sitting with a few people or going to a concert or a gathering can offer you a level of care that you may be looking for. We are not meant to do this life alone. Whatever way feels good to you, go out and be social.

Give Yourself Good Nourishment

There are so many health advisors out there. There are lots of philosophies and fad diets for you to try. Good nourishment is not only the foods you eat but the community you are in; that feeds you too.

Be really kind to yourself and choose what works best for you. Check in with yourself and see if what you are doing is truly caring for yourself.

Care And Others

Creating space for care is a gift for everyone. We can all rise to greater care. Let's start with honoring our feelings and respecting the feelings of others. It always felt strange when I noticed people normalizing and being dismissive of their own feelings and the feelings of others. Isn't this a part of our humanity?

The number of times I've heard people say "fuck those feelings" is alarming. I wondered, is it that we are too afraid to feel? Are we headed in the direction of detaching from a very powerful part of who we are?

What happens if we no longer care about our own feelings or the feelings of the people we love? Where will that lead us?

Even if the mainstream plays down that part of our humanity, I will not. I would not like to fuck my feelings nor the feelings of others. I will embrace, understand, and respect them. That's the least I can do for this God-given ability to feel.

An important note for those of you on the self-care journey, regarding others. You are playing a big game of love and care when you embark on this journey. The company you keep is important. Surround yourself with people who have the ability to respect and honor what you are doing.

Not everyone will be happy for you when you start to make positive changes in your life. You would be surprised at how upset others may get. Some may even try to sabotage you. You may be tempted to self-sabotage.

The fantastic news is that there are people in your life who will honor you and want the best for you.

Change can seem scary for a lot of people. Author Spencer Johnson wrote in his famous book, *Who Moved My Cheese*, "You can believe that a change will harm you and resist it. Or you can believe that finding New Cheese will help you, and embrace the change."[21] And also: "Things change and they are never the same again. This looks like one of those times, Hem. That's life! Life moves on. And so should we."[22]

Encouragement

Initially, I feared what others would do or say and the resistance that took place when I attempted to practice more care for myself. It felt strange and selfish.

The way we care for ourselves is evidence of how well we love ourselves. Caring for ourselves is vital to our well-being and health. Our sense of self-worth is also tied up with care.

How valuable are you to yourself? As a love advocate and believer of the inherent goodness of humanity, I do believe we all are valuable and deserve to be cared for equally.

Walking around unaware and afraid of our feelings and the feelings of others does not allow us to experience life to the fullest. But for those who want to play a bigger game in life and love, I encourage you to lean in. It's time to get even cozier with yourself. Spend time with yourself like you would a love interest. When we are interested in someone, we go out of our way to learn all we can about them. Do that for yourself. I bet there are some beautiful surprises about yourself you didn't even realize.

---

loveWork – Your Opportunity

*The greatest act of self-care is to believe
that we are worthy of care.*
TARA WESTOVER

Self-Care In Action

Purchase a journal or create an e-journal dedicated to self-care. Each day, write how you will care for yourself. The following day, before you write about your next act of self-care, reflect on what you did the day before. Write a reflection on what you discovered.

_____

_____

_____

_____

_____

_____

Example:

October 4th

Today, I'm setting the intention to slow down and reconnect with nature and with myself. I've chosen to take an easy hike for exercise and for presence. There's something healing about being surrounded by trees, breathing in the fresh air, and letting the mind quiet down. I'm giving myself permission to move at my own pace.

October 5th

Yesterday's hike brought me exactly what I needed. I stumbled upon a small waterfall and just sat there, listening. The sound of the water, steady and grounding, helped me tune out the noise in my head. I noticed other people there too, slowing down and being present—and it made me feel connected in a quiet, unspoken way. That peaceful moment stayed with me all day, like a thread of calm running through everything. I slept deeply last night.

Today, I'm choosing connection again, but in a different way. I've made plans to have dinner with a few of my closest friends. Just good food and conversation, no distractions. These kinds of evenings fill me up in a way nothing else does. I'm grateful for the chance to nurture these relationships.

Bonus

Here's a list of self-care activities you can practice. Review the list and circle the ones that interest you.

List of self-care activities:

- Take a walk
- Journal daily
- Take a nap
- Exercise
- Take yourself on a date
- Read a good book
- Unplug from your phone
- Watch a funny movie
- Lay back and listen to music
- Daydream
- Go to your favorite restaurant
- Write a love letter to yourself
- Plan a pampering party
- Make a delicious meal
- Get a massage
- Take a walk in nature
- Get support from a therapist, certified coach, or counselor
- Learn more about self-care from experts
- Spend time with someone you adore
- Take a break from the news outlets and social media
- Go dancing
- Get some extra loving from a loved one or pet
- Join a support group
- Create a bedtime ritual to welcome in a restful night
- Look yourself in the mirror daily and say, "I care about you"
- Create a day dedicated to self-care

List other ways you would like to care for yourself more.

1. _____

2. _____

3. _____

4. _____

5. _____

Chapter 3

Barrier: Lack Of Integrity

To be in integrity is to be one thing, whole and undivided.
MARTHA BECK

Have you played the Jenga game before? Players take turns removing one block at a time from a tower constructed of fifty-four blocks. Each block removed is then placed on top of the tower, creating a progressively more unstable structure. At some point the tower falls and the person who pulled that last block loses.

Recognition Of The Barrier

In my mid-twenties, I had what felt to me like a midlife crisis. It was confusing because I hadn't reached midlife yet. Using the Jenga game metaphor, here's how I would explain it. Throughout my life I tried to carefully stack my life—the Jenga block pieces—neat and sturdy. The blocks were the beliefs about life, goals, career, relationships, all of them. Many of these block pieces were placed by my family, school, church, and society.

As I experienced life for myself outside of what I was taught, my block pieces were pulled out and stacked on top. The world was opening up to me. Some of my beliefs, or what I thought life was, were called into question. The pieces were being moved by a person, a group of people, or an experience.

Eventually, my structure was wobbling. I didn't realize how unstable my stack was until my coworker Rob, now a friend, entered my life. Rob removed the final block. My friendship with Rob was the final Jenga piece that made the whole structure collapse. I didn't see it coming.

There I was, a happy newlywed with a new career at an organization where Rob also worked. Rob is a white, gay male from New Orleans, and I am a Native, Black, heterosexual female from Maryland. We are the same age—our birthdays are weeks apart from each other. Our family background and histories are vastly different. Still, our respective positions at work opened up an opportunity to get to know each other and to develop a friendship.

One of the first things I noticed about Rob was his quiet strength. He was a caring but no-nonsense spitfire with a few sharp edges. Rob had no idea, until this book, that he was the one who inadvertently caused my collapse.

I will never forget the day it happened. Rob and I were in the office copy room, working and talking. By this time, I considered Rob a friend. We hung out outside of work and met each other's family members and friends. For whatever reason, I mentioned some church ideals and wondered out loud about Rob's faith.

The way Rob looked at me, I knew he was about to give me what I came for. "You are not one of those people, are you?" he responded. That question shocked me.

"One of those people?" I asked back.

He answered, "One of those narrow-minded religious people who will tell me I am wrong for the way I am living. A Bible-thumping zealot."

Embarrassed and ashamed, I said, "No," but that wasn't the full truth. I didn't actually know what my truth was.

Rob's question stung. It caused me to check myself.

On my drive home that day I reflected on what happened. I felt bad. My judgment of his lifestyle stripped him of his humanity. I was not a good friend to him.

That night at home I found myself stretched across my bed crying. My interaction with Rob that day caused a reckoning. The block pieces were scattered everywhere. I wasn't in integrity with myself.

I felt split between my own truth and what I was supposed to believe was the truth. This is just one of the many instances where I wasn't living my own truth. I was living how others expected me to.

Some of the things I was taught to believe never quite made sense, but I had accepted them as truth anyway. I was scared to admit it when I didn't agree because I was certain that if I rejected what I'd been taught, the doors of hell would burst wide open and I would head straight in.

The more I thought about where I stood when it comes to gay rights, the truth became evident it didn't bother me. So, if it didn't bother me, then why was I upholding a belief that it's somehow wrong, if I didn't see it as wrong? All I could come up with was that I was afraid of the ridicule for standing as an ally for the LGBTQ+ community.

With respect to all marginalized people, including myself, I want to acknowledge that there are parts of my life where I get to have privilege.

At that point, I also realized that my fear was no longer excusable. I validated my fear but also made a choice to face it. The truth is I am not concerned with nor want to judge people by their sexual orientation. What I wanted was a true and whole friendship with Rob. He deserved the dignity and respect of living out his life's journey.

So, there I was, stretched across my bed, crying quietly because I didn't want to alarm my husband. We were newly married, and I didn't know what Rick would think. The first and only time he had seen me crying was when I was grieving the death of my grandfather, Julius. Then I was able to explain to him why I was crying, but this time I did not know how to explain it. Do I slide him a note that reads, "Baby, I'm having an early life crisis and Rob caused it. Love, your new wife Charmaine"?

Instead, I peeked out of our bedroom to check that he was still watching television in the living room. I quietly grabbed my journal and began to write. Tears followed every word I wrote. There was a story in every tear drop. It seemed like hours had gone by before I truly gathered myself, but it wasn't that long.

Now, I had to find a way to cope while learning how to live in integrity with myself. I didn't think about going to a therapist about it at first. I tried reading some old books I kept but I couldn't get past the first page.

I was grasping for the old me to return because I wasn't sure what would happen if I really did live authentically. After bouts of resistance, I let go of trying to put myself back in the box I was once in. I went through the stages of grief. I was grieving the life that I tried holding on to out of fear.

The grieving process lasted a while. Out of fear, I held on to the resistance to change for a long time. I denied that this was happening. I was angry with myself for being unable to rebuild the scattered pieces anymore. I bargained with God and myself constantly to get over all of this.

I finally reached a place of acceptance—the acceptance that I could no longer live out of integrity with myself. I now had to learn to align with the truth of who Charmaine really is. My friendship with Rob was not the only thing I was out of integrity with.

I no longer wanted to split myself depending on who's around. I believe that integrity is not only doing the right thing even when others aren't looking, but it's also being who you are, no matter what. All I've ever wanted was to be fully accepted for who I am. How ironic, right? So, who am I not to offer that back to another?

I was sick of trying to fit into what everyone else around me was or wanted me to be. I no longer wanted to be in unhappy relationships with people who weren't really good friends to me anyway. I always felt the sincerity of friendship with Rob.

I'd like to say that from that moment on, I lived in integrity, but that would not be true. It took time and patience with myself because change is not always easy. Removing my lack of integrity as a barrier was a challenging task. I had to see all the ways I was out of integrity with myself.

I was also afraid that my change would upset the people in my life, particularly my husband. He was the closest witness to the change. This barrier was huge. It blocked a big portion of my path forward. Despite my fears, I had a burning desire to be me, whole and free.

Understanding Integrity

Our understanding of life and relationships starts at birth. Our particular family system, school, religious practices, and society all play a role. Without placing the blame on any one of those particular systems, I needed to understand where it all came from.

I don't remember the exact incident, but from a young age, I learned how to adapt to situations and circumstances depending on the person involved in order to keep myself safe. It wasn't like I decided one day to be this way. The external pressures, judgment of others, and the fear of not belonging were three of the major reasons for my decision. And when you have the possibility of hell looming over your head for your whole life, it can evoke major fear and anxiety; at least it did for me for half of my life.

Finding my way to my own personal integrity was not about making others wrong or blaming them. I see how everyone was doing the best they could.

I didn't always think this way. We are products of our own family system, school, church, and society. All of those systems are passed down through the generations.

Exploring integrity was quite an adventure. Author of *The Way of Integrity: Finding the Path of Your True Self*, Martha Beck writes, "If you don't walk your true path, you don't find your true people. You end up in places you don't like, learning skills that don't fulfill you, adopting values and customs that feel wrong."[23]

This felt true to me. Beck also encourages her readers to trust their inner teacher above all. Trusting our inner teacher is like a burst of relaxation and freedom that rings through our whole body.

Unhealthy Patterns Of Behavior When Lacking Integrity

Learning how to walk in my truth meant I had to look at the unhealthy patterns I had. Below, I share the patterns that grew the barrier that took on the size of a boulder in my mind's eye. Here's what I found in my research of the unhealthy patterns of behavior.

We Fear Rejection, Judgment, And/Or Conflict

We are pack animals. We want to know we have a place we belong. The desire to fit in can lead to making choices that go against our true selves. Once we feel our first sting of rejection, we never want to feel that ever again.

Being judged by others also stings. And there may be pressure to conform to family expectations, church rules, or societal norms, causing us to suppress our authentic self in favor of what others deem "acceptable."

> We are pack animals. We want to know we have a place we belong. The desire to fit in can lead to making choices that go against our true selves.

We Display Dishonest Behaviors

Hiding parts of ourselves or who we really are to avoid conflict or consequences can damage our sense of self-worth. Lying about who we are or what we believe to stay safe, or even creating a different persona to meet others' expectations, is damaging.

We Follow The Crowd

When we feel pressure to conform and become a group thinker, it takes away our individuality. We suppress our opinions and creativity, ignoring our own inner wisdom.

It takes boldness and courage to stand alone and not succumb to the pressures of particular social norms. Sometimes we think it's easier to go with the majority, even if it doesn't feel right. But in the end we never feel good about it. Understanding and embracing our own perspective can lead to better outcomes.

We Develop Cognitive Dissonance

When we go against what we value, it creates cognitive dissonance. Our behavior does not match our values; it causes internal conflict. That inner conflict can cause anxiety or stress.

It Creates Strained Relationships

Interacting with others while you don't represent your true self can strain relationships. If we feel like we can't show up as our authentic selves, real connection can't happen. When we are dishonest or withholding parts of ourselves, it creates distance in our relationships.

We Experience Stress, Anxiety, And Depression

When we feel like we can't truly be ourselves, it can create inner turmoil. Martha Beck shares in her book, *The Way of Integrity*, "Because our true nature is serious about restoring us to wholeness, it hauls out the one tool that reliably gets our attention: suffering."[24]

Forming New Healthy Patterns With Integrity

Seeing these behaviors in myself helped me understand what to do next. I don't know which one of my teachers taught me the power of staying curious, but it has saved me from placing judgment, blame, or shame on myself or others throughout this journey. I encourage you to stay curious as well.

Build Your Self-Worth And Value Muscle

The fear of rejection, being judged by others, or being in conflict does not feel good. However, we have the ability to rise strong in the face of all.

Understand that your true worth and value are not about what others think but about what you think about yourself. You are the only person who knows who you truly are.

If we adjust our lenses just a bit, rejection is OK. Why would we ever want to be in a place where we're not welcome? Every "no" is leading us to our "yes." Rejoice in the *no's* of life. We don't have to make it mean anything negative about us.

Be Honest With Who You Are

When you hide yourself, you are robbing yourself and others of experiencing your unique, magical self. Think about what everyone is missing out on by not seeing you.

If you are not sure yet, that's OK. It's time you start spending time getting to know yourself.

I hope you rise in love with who you see in the mirror.

Practice Belonging

Dr. Maya Angelou put it best when it comes to understanding belonging. She said in an interview with Bill Moyers, "You only are free when you realize you belong no place—you belong every place—no place at all. The price is high. The reward is great. I belong to myself. I'm very proud of that. I'm very concerned of how I look at Maya. I like Maya very much."[25]

Dr. Brené Brown went further into that exploration in her book, *Braving the Wilderness*, by saying this: "I feel I belong everywhere I go, no matter where it is or who I'm with as long as I never betray myself. Moreover, the minute I become who you want me to be in order to fit in and make sure people like me is the moment I no longer belong anywhere."[26]

> Rejection is OK. Why would we ever want to be in a place where we're not welcome? Every "no" is leading us to our "yes." Rejoice in the *no's* of life. We don't have to make it mean anything negative about us.

Practice Cognitive Consonance

Giving yourself permission to align with your core beliefs and values is a great gift to offer yourself.

If you don't know what they are, it's time to explore what they are.

As you start to live inside your beliefs and values, allow yourself some flexibility to grow and change as you continue to explore life. None of this has to be static. Life is about flow. Find your rhythm of freedom.

Surround Yourself With Harmonious Relationships

Oh, how sweet life is when you are in harmony with the people in your life.

Even when disharmony happens, restoration is possible.

All relationships experience disharmony at some point and more than once. Whether it's with family, friends, or coworkers, we can get back to a place of harmony again. It takes a commitment from all parties involved. There are steps to take, such as maintaining open communication, being honest, taking personal responsibility, being patient, and seeking support from a trusted therapist or coach.

Practice Contentment And Peace

Finding a sense of satisfaction and happiness with life can help with stress, anxiety, and depression.

Keeping a gratitude journal is a great tool.

Also, surround yourself with positive, supportive people and limit exposure to negativity. Being mindful of the energy around you can help maintain a peaceful mind.

Integrity And Others

I've learned the best way to love well is to give the people in my life the dignity and respect of their own path and journey—to allow them to be free to be fully who they are with me. The world can be hard on all of us. We are all trying to figure it out.

Throughout our lives, we've been socialized to fit in in some fashion. Our sense of self-worth and acceptance is challenged almost daily. How our caregivers nurtured our sense of self-worth and acceptance influenced our ability to live in integrity early on. Many of us have been taught in some way to betray or abandon who we are. We do it to win the affection of another, gain a level of status in a career, or out of fear of loss in a relationship. There are so many ways we do this.

Showing up authentically takes courage depending on the situation. If you find yourself in a situation where you feel like you have to betray yourself, please allow yourself to find your way back to personal integrity. No one has the right to ask you to betray who you are for their sake, and the reverse is true. Forcing others to fit in is harmful to our own sense of self-worth and well-being.

Knowing that we belong and living in integrity allows inner peace to settle in. There are plenty of people living in integrity, and they tend to gravitate toward each other. There are people who will love you for exactly who you are. If you already have people who do, cherish it.

Encouragement

The longest and most important relationship you will have is with yourself. I encourage you to stay in integrity with yourself. Splitting or denying any part of yourself causes internal suffering. Before you take your last breath, I hope you get to see your whole and complete brilliance. I hope that others get to experience it as well.

Fair warning: I am a lofty thinker. But, what a beautiful world this would be if we all lived in integrity. I think we have the opportunity to do so. It will take each person committing to show up authentically and allowing others to do the same.

LoveWork—Your Opportunity

Let Your True Self Shine

As you practice living in integrity, please remember to give yourself grace and compassion, offer acceptance, and enjoy the exploration of you. If you are feeling challenged by this LoveWork, please reach out to a trusted therapist, counselor, or credentialed coach for support.

Please write and reflect on the following questions:

Are there area(s) in your life where you are living out of integrity with yourself? If you have identified an area(s) please list it below. (*Example: A friend constantly asks for favors or help, even when you're feeling overwhelmed, and you say "yes" to keep the peace.*)

_____

_____

Based on the areas you have identified, what steps will you take to start living as your authentic self? (*Example: I can be honest with my friend by saying "no" and sharing how our dynamic has affected us.*)

_____

_____

Are there any area(s) of your life where you don't feel like you can be yourself no matter what? If so, what area(s)? *(Example: You might feel like you can't be yourself in a competitive academic or work environment where there is intense pressure to perform.)*

_____

_____

Write why it seems impossible for you to be yourself in that area(s).

_____

_____

Reread what you wrote about the impossibility again slowly. Do you notice a belief you hold about yourself or others? If so, is that belief or story absolutely true? Write your answer.

_____

_____

Can you see where you can let go of that story and practice being in integrity with yourself? Write your answer.

_____

_____

What new steps are you willing to take now?

_____

_____

Bonus

If you dare, here's your opportunity to untangle any knots that keep you and others bound.

Are there ways in which you are forcing someone else to betray themselves for you? If so, who?

_____

_____

_____

_____

Are you willing to forgive yourself and make amends to accept that person for who they are?

_____

_____

_____

_____

Chapter 4

Barrier: **Dishonesty**

There is a price to pay for speaking the truth.
There is a bigger price for living a lie.
CORNEL WEST

D o you remember the first time you told a lie? It could have been about something as simple as taking a cookie from the cookie jar when you weren't supposed to.

Recognition Of The Barrier

Let me take you back to my elementary school days. This is my first recollection of a time when I lied, but I'm sure it wasn't the first time I lied about something. This was an intentional lie I told. I was in third or fourth grade. My classmates and I were standing in line at Mount Harmony Elementary School. Our teacher started at the front of the line and asked us one by one what our religious practices were.

I was close to the back of the line, listening to the responses from my classmates. I kept hearing my classmates say, "Catholic." It seemed like everyone was saying the same thing. I panicked because I didn't remember what religion I was. When she got to me, I quickly said, "Catholic." She moved right along, not even noticing my big fat lie. I knew I wasn't Catholic, nor did I really know any Catholics, except now my classmates. Why on earth did I say "Catholic"?

How do we learn the art of lying? Do we watch the adults in our lives do it? Perhaps. Was it that the world made it confusing because of the contradictions we saw in the behaviors of those we were to trust?

I don't know when lying became a part of my life, but I knew when I was doing it. Sometimes a lie would fly out of my mouth. Even as a young girl, I didn't feel good about lying. Yet, I found myself lying at times. Perhaps my lying began with a cookie jar situation, but it evolved subtly. As a young girl, I often heard this passage of scripture: "When I was a child, I spoke as a child, I understood as a child, I thought as a child; but when I became a man, I put away childish things."[27]

As an adult, I recognize that I am fully responsible for how I live my life. Accessing the barrier of dishonesty and what it would take to move it out of my path didn't seem like a big deal initially. However, upon further examination, there was a bit more girth to this barrier.

What I saw was that withholding and remaining private was a mask for lying. Not saying anything can be deceptive and a form of dishonesty. While I believe privacy should be respected, we can often use it as an excuse to hold on to a lie. Of course, wisdom and discernment come into play when we are deciding what to share about our private business and with whom.

In bell hooks's book *All About Love*, she shares her belief that honesty is one of the ingredients we need to know love. She says, "When men and women punish each other for truth telling we reinforce the notion that lies are better. To be loving we willingly hear each other's truth and, most important, we affirm the value of truth telling. Lies may make people feel better, but they do not help them know love."[28]

In his book, *The Four Agreements*, Don Miguel Ruiz invites us to speak with integrity. His first agreement is to "be impeccable with your word." He invites us into the world of this first agreement by telling us to: "Say only what you mean. Avoid using the word to speak against yourself or gossip about others. Use the power of your word in the direction of truth and love."[29] Taking my time to soak in the teachings of both bell hooks and Don Miguel Ruiz, here's how those patterns of dishonesty showed up in my life.

Understanding Dishonesty

I explored why I told lies, which was an uncomfortable exploration, I might add, because who wants to consider themselves a liar? Yet, there were times I was, whether it was telling someone I was OK when I wasn't or pretending not to care when I did. But if I want to live a life of peace and love, telling lies has to be addressed and removed.

What it all came down to was fear. I feared that if I told the truth, I would be ridiculed, cause conflict, hurt someone's feelings, or lose the relationship, depending on the circumstance and person. I wasn't willing to risk it.

Unhealthy Patterns Of Behavior With Dishonesty

With greater self-awareness, I began paying closer attention to what I shared with others. I started to pick up on when fear crept in, and I was tempted to lie. It was when I was afraid to say what I needed to say.

This practice of honesty requires compassion, grace, and patience. No one is harder on me than I am. So now that I understood that fear was controlling whether I was being honest or not I could now look at the patterns that show up when dishonesty is at play.

What it all came down to was fear. I feared that if I told the truth, I would be ridiculed, cause conflict, hurt someone's feelings, or lose the relationship.

We Avoid Ridicule Or Conflict

When there's tension, it's uncomfortable for most people. Smoothing things over can seem like the best choice. If there is fear of losing the relationship, we lie.

We can often default to lying to protect the feelings of others. The opposite can also be true at times: We may want others to lie to us if we think our feelings will be hurt.

We Try To Escape Punishment

If the outcome is getting into trouble, being criticized, or feeling ashamed, we tend to avoid it by lying. However, it is only a temporary delay of the consequences and can make the issue worse. Eventually, it catches up with us.

We Attempt To Protect Our Self-Image

Do you uphold your righteousness no matter what? Deflecting blame, exaggerating, or pretending to be someone else are unhealthy, dangerous patterns when relating to others. We avoid taking responsibility or looking weak to others at any cost. We can inflate our sense of self as a way to protect our image or to be more favorable than others. We hide parts of ourselves that we believe others won't accept. Sometimes, people lie to project a version of themselves that they think others will accept or admire.

We Want To Spare Someone's Feelings

Sometimes the truth is difficult to share. Sparing someone's feelings seems like a good thing, right? Why would we ever want to hurt someone's feelings?

We think we are protecting the people we care about from harm or disappointment by telling lies, which may seem noble, but it isn't.

We Fear Rejection

One way we justify lying is our faulty thinking that we are being loyal to others. The mere possibility of rejection can scare those who have previously felt its sting into lying to maintain the connection.

However, if the truth is not being told, it hurts or betrays all involved anyway, including yourself.

We Develop A Lack Of Discernment

When it comes to what we share about ourselves to others, lacking the ability to make clear, thoughtful, and wise judgments is irresponsible. Sharing other people's business when you don't know the truth can be damaging. Sharing your own business with people who haven't earned your trust is also irresponsible and damaging for you. Using discernment enables us to distinguish between what is true and what is false. Discernment is a practice of mindfulness that allows us to tap into inner wisdom and intuition.

We Want To Uphold Cultural Or Social Norms

Whether it's cultural, social, or family norms, we tend to lie to uphold agreements with each other. Upholding lies over true connection happens when we are trying to maintain power or control over others.

New Healthy Patterns Of Behavior With Honesty

Self-honesty—not the harsh, critical kind, but the kind that's clear-eyed and grounded is a foundational tool that supports meaningful connections. Psychological research shows that real change happens when we're willing to look at our behavior without sugarcoating or being in denial. When we can name what's truly going on, the areas of the brain responsible for self-control and decision-making are better able to guide our actions. That awareness creates the space for more intentional choices. It's not about being perfect; it's about being real.

Embrace Vulnerability And Confrontation

Whether we like it or not, we experience judgment or criticism from others, including those close to us. Instead of lying to avoid ridicule, allow yourself to be seen for who you truly are, accepting that not everyone may approve or agree with you. Addressing conflicts or difficult situations, knowing that you won't always agree and that you don't have to always agree, helps those involved work through challenges constructively.

> Instead of lying to avoid ridicule, allow yourself to be seen for who you truly are, accepting that not everyone may approve or agree with you.

Reward And Accept Truth Telling

We often wonder what will happen if we do tell the truth. As recounted in the Bible, the truth sets you free. Lying binds you.

When we start rewarding and praising honesty it allows all of us to show up honest and truthful. There are positive outcomes to telling your truth. Making choices that align with your values, earning trust, and acting with integrity lead to positive outcomes rather than punitive ones.

Archbishop Desmond Tutu shared that, "True reconciliation exposes the awfulness, the abuse, the hurt, the truth. It could even sometimes make things worse. It is a risky undertaking but in the end it is worthwhile, because in the end only an honest confrontation with reality can bring real healing. Superficial reconciliation can bring only superficial healing."[30]

Value Yourself

How you love yourself is how you teach others to love you.
RUPI KAUR

How do you see yourself? That's what matters above all. Focusing on your values, self-compassion, and self-care gives you the opportunity to build your self-confidence. Eleanor Roosevelt wisely said, "No one can make you feel inferior without your consent."[31]

Be Yourself

Be yourself; everyone else is already taken.
OSCAR WILDE

If you are reading this book, you may have woken up to the wonder that you are; you would not want to be like anyone else. Take time to get to know yourself and take pride in it, truly. Your brilliance takes nothing away from anyone else.

Be Honest

Telling the truth helps us build and maintain healthy, strong relationships. It also supports our personal growth journey.

Some other benefits of being an honest person include gaining respect, building trust, promoting greater emotional well-being, and reducing stress and anxiety.

Practice Self-Acceptance

Rejection is a part of life.

We can't get around it.

This is why self-acceptance is crucial. When we fully accept ourselves, the need for external validation doesn't play a role when making decisions to tell the truth.

Self-acceptance also builds our confidence muscle. We are able to come back from rejection with resilience, and it could be an opportunity for growth as well.

Make Informed Decisions

Taking our time to carefully assess situations helps when we lack discernment. Critical thinking and emotional intelligence allow us to distinguish between what is true and false, right and wrong, and suspend judgment.

Advocate For Humanity

Cultural, social, and family norms are a delicate topic.

There are aspects of these "norms" that encourage lying to uphold a particular status quo that is harmful to many. Allowing yourself and others to explore new ways of thinking, behaving, or living that go against the status quo is a part of our human rights. Far too often, we cut each other off or worse in order to maintain a norm.

When we can live our lives from our truth without pressure to uphold norms, we can free ourselves and those in our lives. Author Susan David shares, "Courage is not an absence of fear; courage is fear walking."[32]

Each day that we wake up, we get a chance to make a choice toward expansive love for ourselves and others. Removing the barrier of dishonesty widens our path to a happier, healthier life.

The truth is, I didn't want to see this part of myself. I get that what I say and do can invoke love or pain. Being honest in a society, culture, and world that seems to condone lies and deceit is a form of bravery.

Honesty And Others

Commitment to truth-telling lays the groundwork for the openness and honesty that is the heartbeat of love

BELL HOOKS

Do you like to be lied to? No, of course not, none of us likes to be lied to. We get so offended when others lie to us; it's hurtful. We make a big deal about it. However, we turn around and lie to others.

I've met a few people who have professed to have never lied (or hurt) anyone in their lives. I immediately look for the exit door. That is a level of delusion that I'm not interested in participating in.

Holding yourself and others to the truth is a sign of a healthy relationship. We've all had our share of relationship pain around lies and betrayal. It never feels good in the end.

Some are quick to mind the business of others, telling what they believe is the truth, knowing that they really don't know what the truth is. This is another thing we need to be careful of. In American culture, we glorify sharing someone else's business, yet none of us would want that done to ourselves. Through hearsay, we can run off with what we think is true without even knowing a person or having had a conversation with them.

We are all guilty of spreading things we know nothing about. As we practice living honest lives, it also requires us to allow others to share their own business, should they choose to.

Among the most precious gifts of my life are my best friends. I prayed to find these people. My prayer was that I would find people that not only could I be myself with but that I could be honest with about anything: people who would honor my truth, people who would not turn things against me nor use what I tell them in harmful ways toward me, people who would keep my confidence.

My prayers were answered. I've spent over a decade with each of them. We've found safety and trust in each other. We've sat in some uncomfortable moments of truth. Those moments have deepened our relationships with each other.

Grace, compassion, empathy, forgiveness, and sheer acknowledgement of our humanity come into play when we are in the truth-telling business. I wish that for all of us.

Encouragement

Authenticity is a collection of choices that we have to make every day. It's about the choice to show up and be real. The choice to be honest. The choice to let our true selves be seen.

BRENÉ BROWN

My hope is that you all find yourselves in relationships where honesty is valued, where you are safe to speak your truths, and where your truth heals and frees you from any suffering you may be in.

loveWork–Your Opportunity

Be Impeccable With Your Word

Author Don Miguel Ruiz, along with Janet Mills, writes,

> The first and most important of The Four Agreements is to be impeccable with your word. The word is your power of creation, and that power can be used in more than one direction. One direction is impeccability, where the word creates a beautiful story—your personal heaven on earth. The other direction is misuse of the word, where the word destroys everything around you, and creates your personal hell.[33]

Over the next week, be mindful of the way you speak to yourself and about others. Pay attention to what you are saying. Do you mean what you are saying? Are you gossiping about others?

At the end of each day, write in your journal your reflection of how impeccable with your words you were.

Bonus

Your Personal Commitment To Honesty

Being honest with yourself is the first and most important step. This act is personal and sacred. Take some time to write a commitment statement to yourself. Below is an example.

My Commitment To Honesty And Self-Compassion

I commit to building a meaningful and loving relationship with myself and my community, rooted in truth and integrity. I will practice being honest with myself and with others, even when it feels uncomfortable or difficult. I will choose to trust my inner voice first, knowing that self-trust is the foundation of all authentic connection. I will meet myself with compassion and gentleness, releasing the need for perfection. In every step, I will honor my growth, stay grounded in honesty, and lead with love.

_____

_____

_____

_____

_____

Note: This practice is to support you in living freely. Please don't judge what you notice. If you do notice that you need to work on this area and need support, please reach out to a trusted therapist or coach.

Chapter 5

Barrier: Lack Of Emotional Safety

The last bit of any sense of emotional safety went completely away shortly after my husband, Rick, died. For a good portion of my life, I didn't feel supported emotionally. I had no idea what to do with my emotions or how others could help me figure it out.

Recognition Of Barrier

In my teenage years, I hit some rough patches. Like most teenagers, my emotions were all over the place. In middle school, my best friend at the time and I had this idea to write in notebooks about what's going on in our lives and swap the notebooks so we could read and respond. I shared all my secrets and thoughts with her.

Then my parents ended up with my notebook. My friend had shared my private business with other friends and my parents. I was crushed, and of course, I got into trouble.

That was my first experience of a betrayal like that.

Shortly after that, a guy I went to church with called me. He is a year or two older than me. This should have been a sign he was up to something because we weren't friends. He must have known somehow that I held another person's secret. He insisted that I tell him and that he would keep the secret too. I was holding strong, but he was persistent, saying things like, "You can trust me."

Against my better judgment, I gave in. He turned right around and told everyone what I shared and spun it so that I looked like the big mouth. He left out the part of what he said and did to get the information out of me. I trusted no one after that.

Besides my grandparents, I didn't know who I could trust. Those experiences shaped my belief that I wasn't safe emotionally. Because my emotional safety was compromised at an early age, I felt insecure, criticized, and rejected.

While I tried to keep my separation from my husband discreet and not share our business, it seems my husband did not. Two of Rick's friends called me on separate occasions and shared that he said some pretty bad things about me.

One tried encouraging me to leave the area, saying no one liked me anymore. He said, "Rick said some really bad things about you." I felt betrayed by Rick, too, the one person in the world I had bonded with most. All the pain of the past came back to join the unbearable pain I was experiencing from losing him. Mourning him became complicated. I questioned who we were. The one person I believe I loved more than anyone else on this planet was gone, and the aftermath and drama behind his death left me feeling unsafe.

Rick's death was a catalyst to deep healing and awakening. I choose to confront everything, including this idea of safety. The best advice I received was from my mentor Katherine Woodward Thomas. Thomas said, "Don't look at the situation as a victim." She invited me to look at the choices I made and take responsibility for those choices. That's where I would find my freedom. She also said even if we believe the other person was 97 percent wrong, we have to own our 3 percent and focus on that.

Of course, I wasn't responsible for the decision that others made, but I made a choice as well. While I know Rick was not 97 percent responsible for where we ended up in our marriage, my intent, even before he died, was to own my part fully. I was already working on this prior to his passing. I had enrolled in a class and was working on showing up better in our relationship. I shared with him what I was doing. He was aware of the strides I was trying to make.

What I realize is that I hadn't cultivated an emotionally safe relationship with myself first. This whole time I was looking for others to keep me safe emotionally when I wasn't attempting to keep myself safe. It wasn't fair of me to want others to keep me safe when I couldn't do it myself. It also wasn't fair to them when they didn't know how to do it for themselves, either.

Understanding Emotional Safety

We learn a lot in elementary school through high school, but learning about our soft skills is not one of them. Emotional education was not one of the subjects I ever had.

Of course, in college, if you studied psychology, sociology, or another related field, you gained insight into human behavior. This is why I believe that getting support from well-trained and trusted professionals can help you transform your life. With the help of my coaches and therapists, I got a better understanding of how to work with the emotional safety barrier.

Unhealthy Patterns Of Behavior For Emotional Safety

My childhood experiences, unhealthy relationships with others throughout my life, trauma, social pressures, fear of rejection, and lack of trust were stacked on each other to create this barrier. Because of my belief that I wasn't emotionally safe with anyone, I formed unhealthy patterns of behavior. Here's what I found in my research of what shows up when this barrier is present.

We Emotionally Shut Down

When we don't feel emotionally safe, we will avoid situations, withdraw from conversations, or shut down all of our feelings. We tend to avoid people or situations that make us feel uncomfortable.

We Overcompensate In Many Situations

There could be several different reasons why the pattern of overcompensating shows up. It could be due to fear of rejection, social pressures, a need for control, insecurity, or a desire to be accepted.

It tends to show up as people-pleasing as well. Oftentimes, we suppress our own feelings, needs, and desires in favor of trying to maintain a sense of safety.

We Act Disingenuous

We tend to show up in ways that are not consistent with our true selves in order to remain safe. We are not authentic or genuine when relating to others. It tends to make us feel empty, sad, or depressed because we suppress our true identity.

We Emotionally Detach

When we don't feel emotionally safe, we tend to suppress our feelings. This detachment or suppression is our way of trying to protect ourselves from the perceived harm. Sharing our true feelings is out of the question at that point.

We Overthink

Oftentimes, we find ourselves replaying situations in our minds, trying to figure out what happened, what went wrong. We tend to worry, which in turn causes us to feel anxious. This is a sign we are trying to find our way back to safety. There's a fear of being judged or rejected underneath all of it.

We Are Overly Critical Of Ourselves

Do you have a harsh inner critic? Most of us do. Our inner critic points out how inadequate we are and highlights all our mistakes. This leads to insecurity and a feeling of unworthiness.

We Find It Difficult To Trust Others

Where there is a lack of trust, we struggle to feel safe with others. We find it difficult to open up for fear of betrayal, rejection, or judgment. We avoid being vulnerable.

New Healthy Patterns Of Behavior Of Emotional Safety

Despite my past experiences and the fear they left behind, I deeply longed for an authentic connection with both myself and others, where emotional safety could truly exist. I wanted to feel safe not only in my relationships but within my own body and mind. As I began to examine the unhealthy behavioral patterns I had developed as a way to protect myself, I started to see how those old strategies, while once necessary, were now holding me back. Gaining that insight gave me space to try something different. As I slowly began to build emotional safety from within, I noticed a shift: my nervous system began to settle, and I started to feel a sense of inner calm I hadn't known before.

Here's what I found in my research about what it really takes to form healthy patterns that support emotional safety.

Practice Expressing Yourself

As we learn more about how we feel and understand our feelings, we can then move on to expressing ourselves to others. Sharing your feelings and thoughts can be scary at first, but start a little at a time.

Self-reflecting by journaling can be a powerful tool to use as you practice expressing yourself. If you need support, seek a trusted professional who can work with you.

Maintain Balance

Overcompensating and people-pleasing are our ways of trying to make up for perceived shortcomings. To counteract this, self-acceptance is key. Letting go of the need to prove ourselves to others by staying grounded and resisting the urge to go over the top for others will help us find emotional safety within ourselves.

Practice Authenticity

Honoring our true selves is essential on this journey of happy, healthy living. Taking off your mask to see yourself is important. Embrace and align with your values without the need for approval from others.

Learn How To Securely Attach

Our goal is to establish a secure attachment to ourselves and others. The practice of secure, healthy emotional attachment always starts with us first. It's through self-awareness, being with our own emotions, and connecting with others authentically that we can create a safe container in relationships. Healthy, safe attachments include empathy, compassion, and grace.

Practice Being Present

It can be difficult to stay in the present moment when we tend to overthink situations. We may be present physically, but mentally, we are already trying to assess what's really going on.

The practice of being present with what's happening in the moment helps us stay away from being carried away in our own stories or interpretations of what's going on. Oftentimes, we find that there's nothing to fear.

> The practice of secure, healthy emotional attachment always starts with us first. It's through self-awareness, being with our own emotions, and connecting with others authentically that we can create a safe container in relationships.

Practice Self-Compassion

Compassion is genuine. It's rooted in care, kindness, and concern. When we understand our humanness, compassion fills our hearts. Author of *Real Love: The Art of Mindful Connection*, Sharon Salzberg, shares, "Compassion grows in us when we know how the energy of love is available all around us." She also shares that compassion does not make us weak. It's a powerful cognitive experience both with yourself and others.[34]

Build Trust With Yourself

Growing our trust muscle happens when we learn to trust ourselves first. Slowing down to listen to our intuition and then going with what it says will build that muscle.

Being honest with yourself and others is another way to build it. Self-reflection is a good tool here when trust is broken. Take the time to reflect on what happened and what you can do moving forward.

Safety And Others

Prioritizing our well-being, advocating for ourselves, and building a strong, healthy community are ways we learn emotional safety. It's crucial to create emotional safety with yourself first.

Once we understand how to do it, we can also offer emotional safety within our community. Children have no way of knowing what to do when they don't feel emotionally safe, so it's critical to show them how by being safe with them. We are in a mental health crisis. Getting the support we need to learn how to maintain a healthy, sound mind is self-care and love.

At the height of not feeling safe at all once Rick passed, I shut the world out. During my grief, I spent a lot of time reading, journaling, meditating, taking classes, and getting support from both my coaches and therapist. My desire was to allow love to teach me everything I needed to know.

Once I thought I had gotten the hang of learning how to be safe within myself, I started to engage with a small group of people, and then more people. I knew it wasn't going to be easy or perfect. But I quickly learned it's one thing to know something and another to put it into practice.

There were times I went against my intuition. My old patterns were showing up. I couldn't believe it. But I remembered author and psychotherapist Esther Perel shared in her book, that it is in relationship with others that we learn and are able to access how we are doing. Building relationships with others can't happen alone. Perel says, "The more we trust, the farther we are able to venture."[35]

There are people who have not found safety within themselves yet, so they tend to be unsafe with others. It can be devastating to experience the betrayal of others. What's important is that we learn how to recover well, enforce boundaries, and don't give up. There are people who are safe and with whom you can explore life.

Encouragement

Emotional safety is vital for our well-being. When we don't feel safe, we act it out in so many harmful ways. Making the choice to rise in love requires us to show up for ourselves in ways we never have before. The more you practice being emotionally safe with yourself, the more you will create safety around you. Inner peace is possible.

Please reach out to a trusted professional for assistance if needed.

> Emotional safety is vital for our well-being. When we don't feel safe, we act it out in so many harmful ways.

LoveWork—Your Opportunity

*Do not let anything that happens in life be important enough
that you're willing to close your heart over it.*
MICHAEL A. SINGER

Self-Reflection

Take some time to answer these questions:

In what ways will I learn to express myself? (*Examples: journal about my feelings, take a course on communication, or talk to a trusted therapist or coach.*)

_____

_____

What are some things I will practice to maintain balance? (*Examples: focus on taking care of myself, check my motives, and set boundaries.*)

_____

_____

How can I practice being more authentic? (*Examples: get to know myself more through journaling, embrace my emotions, speak my truth, and align with my values.*)

_____

_____

What steps can I take to develop a secure emotional attachment? (*Examples: get intimate with myself, learn effective communication skills, and build self-trust.*)

_____

_____

How can I practice being present? (*Examples: bring myself back to the present moment each time my mind wanders off, check the stories running through my head, and practice meditation.*)

_____

_____

What can I do to practice more self-compassion? (*Examples: allow myself to feel, speak kindly to myself, and treat myself like a best friend.*)

_____

_____

What can I do to practice trusting myself? (*Examples: listen to my intuition, pay attention to how I'm feeling, and embrace and learn from my mistakes.*)

_____

_____

Bonus

Based on your answers, write below what you could start to practice to ensure others feel safe with you.

_____

_____

_____

_____

_____

Chapter 6

Barrier:
Resentment

*The difference between real acceptance and
just backing away from an issue,
or away from the whole relationship, is resentment.*

TERRENCE REAL

Resentment is one of those emotions I didn't think was a barrier for me. But I ran right into that barrier.

Addressing these things isn't fun. I harbored resentment for the hurt and disappointment I couldn't express to the people I had grievances against.

Recognition Of The Barrier

It all came to a boiling point in 2022.

I was at the angry stage of the grieving process. I was hopping mad at everything and everyone for the way I was treated. There's no way for me to go through every grievance in this chapter, but I could taste the feeling of bitterness starting to manifest. I was going in the wrong direction, heading down that path.

I pulled out my journal and began to work it out on paper. I didn't hold back on how I was feeling. Everything was coming up. There it was in plain sight, all of it. At least everything I could remember.

Now that I was aware of it, I needed to find ways to dismantle this barrier. Resentment is not the energy I want to carry within me and into all my relationships. Resentment doesn't appear overnight and can be a silent killer in relationships. It's built on a foundation of behaviors that go unchecked for too long.

Resentment is a complex emotion that can develop when we feel wronged, overlooked, or disrespected in our relationships. It often arises when our needs, desires, or boundaries are not being acknowledged or respected, leaving us with feelings of bitterness, anger, or frustration. The roots of resentment may lie in unexpressed grievances, unmet expectations, or patterns of repeated emotional hurt.

Unlike temporary irritation, resentment is deep-seated and festers over time, making it harder to release without conscious effort.

When we leave conflict unresolved, it slowly erodes safety and trust. If we find ourselves participating in passive-aggressive behavior or withdrawing emotionally or physically, resentment may be present.

Resentment doesn't happen because of a single event; it develops as time passes. Often, it's not just the immediate problem that causes resentment, but it's the past resentments that have been simmering and building pressure. When one or both people in the relationship feel ignored, unheard, unappreciated, or unseen, it compounds the emotional buildup.

Resentment is deep-seated and festers over time, making it harder to release without conscious effort.

Unhealthy Patterns Of Behavior When Resentment Is Present

When resentment takes root, it often fuels a cycle of unhealthy behavior that keeps us emotionally stuck. We may begin to withdraw from others, using silence as a weapon or avoidance as a shield. Passive-aggressive communication, sarcasm, or subtle sabotage can become default modes of expression, all while denying our true feelings. Over time, this emotional armor distorts our perception, making it difficult to see others—or ourselves—clearly. Instead of addressing the underlying hurt, we may replay past offenses, justifying bitterness and reinforcing our victimhood. These patterns not only damage our relationships but also drain our energy and block personal growth. Recognizing and interrupting these behaviors is the first step toward emotional freedom and genuine healing.

We Avoid Difficult Conversations

Learning how to communicate is a soft skill we all need to continue to expand. Difficult conversations are uncomfortable, but for the health of the relationship, it's crucial. When issues are swept under the rug instead of being addressed, they build up over time, and resentment becomes unavoidable. At that point, it may seem impossible to address.

We Suppress Our Emotions

Unexpressed emotions don't eventually go away; they continue to bubble up, grow, and fester until addressed.

Staying quiet doesn't work. Allowing self-expression when it comes to dealing with our emotions helps us understand ourselves first. We don't always have to express ourselves to others; we can be our own outlet.

We Develop A Sense Of Entitlement
When there is a belief that we are entitled to specific behaviors in a relationship, and those expectations are not met, the seed of resentment is planted. In many cases, it's unspoken expectations or agreements, as well as unrealistic expectations, that create resentment.

We Lack Accountability
The dynamics of relationships involve all parties. When we are not willing to take responsibility for our behaviors and actions, then resentment builds. If we continuously blame everyone else for how the relationship is going, it creates a major imbalance. The scale of unfairness will eventually tip the relationship over.

We Become Self-Sacrificing
Being the martyr in any relationship is unhealthy and handicaps the relationship. Giving up the joys in your life for another leads to resentment and bitterness. Consistently giving up your desires, needs, or comfort for the sake of the relationship is unhealthy.

Healthy Patterns To Counter Resentment
Resentment can quietly erode our well-being, distorting our actions and relationships if left unchecked. Recognizing the unhealthy patterns it creates and actively choosing healthier responses is key to breaking free. Rather than allowing bitterness to build, we must learn to identify our emotions, take responsibility for our reactions, and communicate our needs with honesty and clarity. When we consciously shift our behavior, we not only protect our peace but also create space for healing, understanding,

and deeper connection with others. Through my research, I've identified several effective ways to counter these unhealthy patterns and begin the process of emotional repair.

Build Your Communication Skills

If you have a hard time with difficult conversations, it's OK to get support. Having open and honest communication builds trust, creates safety, and can deepen the bond. Learning to address your issues as they arise instead of allowing them to fester gives you and the other person a chance to work through the situation in real time so that you can move forward with life peacefully.

> Learning to address your issues as they arise instead of allowing them to fester gives you and the other person a chance to work through the situation in real time so that you can move forward.

Set Healthy Boundaries

Setting healthy, clear boundaries keeps everyone safe. Respecting each other's limits, both partners can maintain their sense of self while also nurturing the relationship. It is also a kind thing to do in relationships.

Acknowledge And Validate Your Emotions As Well As Others'

We all have the right to our emotions. It's a part of our human experience; it's intel that helps us navigate through life. Of course, we want to find balance so that we're not overly identified with our emotions. When we overly identify with our emotions, we stop seeing them as temporary experiences and start believing they define us. This can cloud our judgment and lead to reactive behavior, especially with emotions like resentment or anger. Instead of responding thoughtfully, we act from a place of pain.

Suppressing our feelings is never a good idea. Cultivating healthy relationships involves acknowledging and validating each other's emotions. We want to create safety by making sure we don't dismiss our feelings or the feelings of others.

Share In Each Other's Growth

Healthy relationships thrive when all parties choose to take responsibility for their actions and the health of the relationship. The willingness to work together to solve problems is generous and keeps the seed of resentment from being planted.

Show Appreciation

Saying "thank you" costs us nothing, however, it goes a long way in relationships. There are several studies that suggest there are positive effects that gratitude has on the brain. There are also several studies on the positive effects of relationships and how couples tend to grow when they actively show appreciation and gratitude.

Resentment and Others

Resentment doesn't just stay confined to romantic relationships—it affects all the relationships of our lives including the workplace. Because of its subtlety, it can create toxic environments when not addressed.

When resolving resentment, it requires mutual effort, reciprocity, and respect, and when those qualities are one-sided, the emotional imbalance becomes palpable. It's so important to express yourself when challenges arise.

When resentment is present in family relationships, especially when one sibling or spouse consistently assumes the role of the peacemaker, swallowing frustration to maintain peace can be damaging for all involved. The same can be true in the workplace. If you are the one carrying the load for your colleagues, it's just as damaging.

Cultivating an environment of fairness, recognition, and open communication is an effective way to prevent resentment from arising. When people feel valued, acknowledged, and appreciated, relationships have a chance to flourish.

It's important to address resentment in our community. There's a lot of resentment that is festering when we look at it from the broader context in the United States. Resentment is a silent force dividing groups. When people feel excluded, misunderstood, or there's preferential treatment, resentment is alive and well.

We thrive on inclusion, transparency, and respect, and when these elements are missing, it's easy for destructive behaviors to take root. Resentment tears us apart.

Encouragement

Letting go of resentment is one of the most powerful and freeing gifts you can give yourself, even though I know it can feel nearly impossible. That heavy weight of bitterness, that lingering anger, feels so justified when we've been hurt. But holding on to it only chains you to the past, draining your energy and peace.

Picture how much lighter your heart would feel if you could finally release that burden, if you could step into a life where joy, love, and calm can flow freely. You *deserve* that. You deserve to feel the freedom that comes with forgiveness—not for them, but for you.

Forgiveness isn't about excusing the hurt or forgetting it; it's about choosing to no longer let it control you. You have the power to release that pain and step into the freedom that comes with it.

You are worthy of lightness, of peace, of joy—and you have every right to embrace it. Let go, because you are worth every ounce of healing and every moment of peace that follows.

LoveWork–Your Opportunity

One Step At A Time

Please answer the questions below. Please reach out to a trusted therapist, counselor, or credentialed coach to help you through this process if you are challenged by the exercise.

Is there anyone whom you resent? If so, what happened?

_____

_____

How long have you been holding on to that resentment?

_____

_____

Would you like to release it? If yes, which healthy pattern will you start with? If not, what are you getting out of holding on to the resentment? (If you're not ready, it's OK, just understand why you're not ready.)

_____

_____

Imagine how you would feel if you let go of that resentment? Write how you might feel once you are free from it.

_____

_____

Bonus

Write a letter of appreciation to yourself about how proud you are of doing really hard things. Once you are done with the letter, do something you enjoy. Take it easy.

Chapter 7

Barrier:
Forgiveness

Forgiveness is not a choice you make for someone else;
it is a choice you make for yourself . . .
Forgiveness is rarely easy, but it is always possible.
DESMOND AND MPHO TUTU

*I*t is with great respect that I broach this topic.

This chapter is written differently from the other chapters. I am not an expert on forgiveness, but I went to the experts to help me work through the major obstacles I had when it came to forgiveness.

There was really no way around addressing the sacred act of forgiveness if I wanted to experience real love and connection. Much like going through the grief process, it's not something you can skip over.

I had a lot of angst around sharing my personal journey to forgiveness because I would have to address some experiences that affect my loved ones, namely my parents, whom I love and have found forgiveness with.

113

As a young girl, I learned that in the Black community we don't talk about intimate things like abuse, trauma, neglect, or even healing. As an adult, it seems this is a problem across cultures. We don't talk about our pain. We've learned to suffer in silence. There are often one or two wild cards within each family who will go there and want restitution. In a lot of cases these family members get reprimanded, disowned, made to look crazy, or have to distance themselves from their family to keep themselves safe.

My journey to forgiveness began many years ago. There were a few things I was still grappling with years later that I didn't know how to work through. I wanted to let it go and move forward, but I felt stuck in the hurt and pain of it.

I began by researching what thought leaders, spiritual leaders, and scientific studies had to say about forgiveness. I was motivated by what I was learning. Applying what I was learning was going to be the key to my breakthrough.

The Book of Forgiving, by Archbishop Desmond Tutu and his daughter Mpho Tutu, was the catalyst for my breakthrough.[36] It took me two years to get through that book. Not because it was a thick book, but because of the way they were inviting us into the active practice of forgiving. I would pick up the book and then have to set it down because I was just not ready for this level of maturity, nor did I have the courage. As author and activist James Baldwin said, "Love does not begin and end the way we seem to think it does. Love is a battle, love is a war; love is a growing up."[37]

The Tutus' teaching about forgiveness felt too vulnerable, confronting, and scary. Yet it also offered the biggest form of compassion and grace for all of humanity. Their wisdom and insight were nothing like I'd ever heard before. It is love in action.

The stories they share in the book about how they themselves walked through forgiveness, as well as those of other people, changed my heart forever. It fanned the flames in my heart to continue to create a healthy, loving community.

Turning the other cheek was how I learned forgiveness. It was passive, with little to no reconciliation. It was a basic apology, and then the parties moved on. No amends were made in order to restore a sense of goodwill to do better moving forward.

Was the person who was offended really OK? Did the offender truly understand how hurtful their actions were? Could things ever go back to the way it was? Could they really start over? I suppose it depends on the individuals involved and the nature of the offense that occurred.

The Tutus believed that there is nothing that cannot be forgiven and there is nobody that is undeserving of forgiveness.

That statement alone was a tough pill for me to swallow. I was challenged by my own self-righteousness about what and who deserves forgiveness. Of course, there were things that were just unforgivable, right? Or were there?

Needing to let go of my own self-righteousness is why it took me two years to get through the book. Like all the other blocks or obstacles that kept me from love, I needed to check myself. Learning to sit in the seat of forgiveness was so uncomfortable. Reading the book made me angry, sad, and hopeful. This barrier was my most challenging.

Working through my particular process of forgiveness was quite emotional for me. I had to take my time working through it. My therapist, coaches, and wise mentors helped me along the way, and they still do.

> The Tutus believed that there is nothing that cannot be forgiven and there is nobody that is undeserving of forgiveness.

Eventually, my heart began softening to our shared humanity. Now I understand what's so amazing about grace. In time, I was able to let myself and others off the hook, which was a big sigh of relief.

There were two things I needed to let go of: the need to be right and the role of the victim. I don't think I am a black-and-white thinker, but in those instances, I was. I lacked understanding of how free I could be if I forgave myself and others. And it was my unwillingness to forgive that made it hard for me to truly connect with myself and others in healthier ways.

It was costing me to lose the precious time I had on this earth to be with the people I love.

Once that realization sunk in, I started putting the forgiveness practice into action. There was no way I wanted to waste any more time. Also, I believe that one of the best ways to show gratitude for my life is to love to the best of my ability.

> It was my unwillingness to forgive that made it hard for me to truly connect with myself and others in healthier ways. It was costing me to lose the precious time I had on this earth to be with the people I love.

The fourfold path of forgiveness from *The Book of Forgiving* was the format I used. In their book, the Tutus also share the alternative to this fourfold path, which is the revenge cycle. The revenge cycle leaves us perpetually in pain and brings harm, violence, and cruelty. I think it's worth sharing that cycle as well.

The revenge cycle looks like this:

- Violence and cruelty

- Hurt, harm, and loss

- Pain

- Choosing harm

- Rejecting shared humanity

- Revenge, retaliation, and payback

And the cycle repeats itself, like being on a hamster wheel.

The forgiveness cycle fourfold path is:

- Tell the story (to someone safe)

- Name the hurt

- Grant forgiveness (recognizing the shared humanity)

- Renew or release the relationship

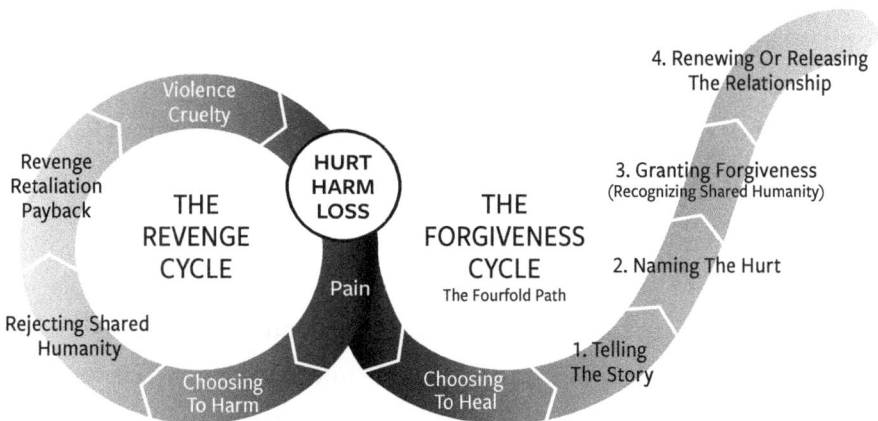

Walking the path of the forgiveness cycle, I noticed that anger became a close companion to my fear. I had not allowed myself to express my anger fully, but it showed up throughout the forgiveness cycle. The anger stemmed from all the ways in which I was hurt and, in turn, how I hurt others. Katherine Woodward Thomas, my wise mentor, once said anger is a sign that something needs to change.

There were moments of frustration. My inner critic was speaking very loudly, saying things like: "Why do you put yourself through this stuff? Why can't you just leave well enough alone?"

Sharon Salzberg teaches us how to speak to our inner critic lovingly.[38] So my way of speaking to her went like this, "Sweetheart, it's time to do this. There's no way around it. Everything will be OK. I know this is scary, but I will do my very best to keep us safe." I've had to reassure my inner critic of this many times because she's strong-willed.

At the beginning of this forgiveness journey, there was some unlearning I had to do. As I mentioned before, the way I was taught to forgive was superficial and passive.

Throughout my life, it seemed like the burden to carry the offense of what happened was laid on the victim. It seemed as if the perpetrator or offender got a pass or a slap on the hand. The shame and even guilt were often held by the person who suffered the offense. Oftentimes, the perpetrator or offender was somehow supported by others. One too many times I watched the victim be shamed, ignored, or even blamed for the aggression that happened.

The biggest breakthrough was forgiving my parents, all four of them. This took some time and patience to sort all of it out. Our parents are the first gateway to understanding love. So, my understanding of love was how I was cared for by them. No matter how present my grandparents were, my parents' love made the biggest impression on me.

I had held on to a belief that my parents should already have had it all together. My biological parents were finishing up high school when

I came along. They weren't ready to become parents. Our age difference was the same as that of siblings in some cases. They had a lot of growing up to do themselves while trying to raise me. My stepparents were close to the same age as my parents, so they had growing up to do as well. As a young girl, I had no concept of that, I just felt unwanted by them.

Things were messy among them. Being an only child among the four of them wasn't fun.

Getting through all the heavy stuff of feeling unloved by them was no small feat. I took my time and learned how to be gentle with myself first. I knew I reached true forgiveness when I no longer needed my parents to change for me to truly be happy. I didn't need history to be rewritten for me to be OK.

My renewed relationship with them feels like a miracle, not perfect by any means, but a miracle just the same.

Both sets of parents kicked me out of their house when I was nineteen. My relationship with them was strained for many years. I became fiercely independent, keeping them at a distance. Allowing myself to heal and create a new relationship with them was scary. I wasn't sure if I could do it. There are still some minor bumps in the road, but we're getting through it.

Along the way, there was another aspect to this healing that needed to be addressed. I developed painful beliefs as a young girl that I was unlovable, not ever good enough, unwanted, and would always be alone, based on how I was treated.

In her book *Conscious Uncoupling*, Katherine Woodward Thomas helped me understand that we create that first wounding from the first heartbreak we feel as a young child.[39] When that first heartbreak happens, it creates a "source fracture story," the false belief about ourselves. Those false beliefs get played out over and over again until we become conscious of them and break the pattern.

This insight was another life-changing moment for me. I saw all the ways in which I was reliving the painful patterns based on what I believed.

Today, I know I am lovable, more than good enough, wanted, and never alone. However, there are times when I find myself collapsing into one of those false beliefs about myself when I get triggered. I've put in a lot of practice so I know how to get myself back to the truth of who I am.

As my heart began to soften through the forgiveness path, I could see my parents' humanity. I could see that they love me the best way they know how. And I am more than willing to love them back to the best of my ability. They were once children who dealt with disappointments and hurts as well.

We are all doing the best we can. The best I can do is respect their individual journey in this life and keep taking care of my well-being. Everything else will take care of itself. It took me a long time to get here, but I made it. There is nothing left to forgive.

After experiencing what it feels like to forgive versus not forgive, I will continue to choose forgiveness every time. I can attest that it's not always easy, but it's possible. I am forever grateful that I gave myself a chance at happiness, love, connection, and freedom.

Forgiveness And Others

. . . first, do no harm.
HENRY MARSH

There is no way I can not offer forgiveness when I, too, have needed to be forgiven. Asking for forgiveness is brave. Admitting when we've done someone wrong is courageous. To sit and listen to someone share their experience with you about how you've hurt them without getting defensive requires a certain level of emotional maturity. Making amends is love in action.

The last step in the forgiveness cycle is deciding to release or renew the relationship; it's a part of the journey. With either decision, love can still be very present.

None of us is perfect. We will not get it right every time, and that's OK. Every time I've had to ask for forgiveness and let the person know how I plan to show up better somehow deepens my love and commitment to them.

Our country has a major reckoning to deal with when it comes to how we deal with righting wrongs and injustices. This is the case especially when it comes to Native and Black Americans, people of color, and other marginalized communities. It is insulting and inhumane to expect us to passively brush things off, or be forced to swallow our feelings. So many have been pushed to just move on and suffer in silence. When we are forced or coerced to "forgive," it strips us of our humanity. We've all witnessed or have been affected by some pretty egregious behavior that affects all of us.

It's important to understand that not everyone will want to lean into forgiveness. I've been met with resistance around even having hard conversations when things are tough. If someone is unwilling or not capable of working through the forgiveness journey with you, you can do it without them. Remember, forgiveness is for you.

Encouragement

Forgiveness is possible. Please be gentle with yourself as you figure out the best approach to take toward peace and freedom. This is a sacred time of healing. Please treat it as such. Honor your humanity; no one is perfect. Each day, we have a chance to make things better for ourselves until our time on earth is done.

LoveWork—Your Opportunity

If you are ready to take steps toward forgiveness, please seek the support of a trusted therapist or certified coach. Oftentimes, we seek out advice from family or friends who are well-meaning, but this is a time of healing that needs to be carefully tended to and will take some time. Take good care of yourself in this process.

Forgiveness Exercise. *Honoring My Forgiveness Journey*
Begin by creating a calm space for reflection. Breathe deeply, ground yourself, and when you're ready, respond to the prompts below from a place of truth and self-compassion.

> ### *Example Of The Forgiveness Cycle:* *Fourfold Path*
>
> *Scenario:* One friend found out that another friend had shared something of theirs with others that was confidential.
>
> **The One Who Was Hurt (The Offended):**
> Tell a story (to the offending friend, or alternatively to someone safe):
>
> "[Friend's name], I shared something personal with you in confidence, and you told others. That was meant to stay between us. When you broke that trust, it really hurt me."
>
> **Name The Hurt:**
> "I already struggle with trusting people, so this experience only deepens that fear. It affected more than just me—it hurt my family too."

Grant Forgiveness:

"I'm not fully there yet, but I'm willing to take steps toward forgiving you because I don't want to carry this pain forever."

Renew Or Release The Relationship:

Renew: "I'll need some time, but I'd like to rebuild our friendship, starting fresh."

Release: "I've decided to let go of our friendship here. I still wish you well."

The One Who Caused Harm (The Offender):

Tell the story (to the hurt person or someone safe):

"[Friend's name], I'm sorry for betraying your trust. I shared something you told me in confidence, and I know that was wrong. You have every right to feel hurt."

Name The Hurt:

"I see that I broke your trust. I caused pain not only to you but also to those close to you. That wasn't fair, and I own that."

Make Amends:

"If you're open to it, I'd like to work on rebuilding trust between us. I will not repeat this mistake. I'll protect what's shared with me going forward—not just for you, but with everyone. I'm here to listen—please let me know what you need to feel safe again."

Renew Or Release The Relationship:

Renew: "Thank you for giving me another chance. I'm committed to earning back your trust."

Release: "I respect your decision if you choose not to continue this relationship. I'm still sorry, and I'll carry this lesson forward."

Who is someone I still feel pain or resentment toward? What happened that still feels unresolved?

_____

_____

What exactly do I need to forgive them for? (Be specific.)

_____

_____

How is holding on to this hurt affecting my life or my peace?

_____

_____

What might change in my heart, body, or spirit if I chose to forgive—even if they never apologize?

_____

_____

Do I want to renew this relationship, or is it healthier for me to release it? Why?

_____

_____

Is there anyone I've hurt, intentionally or not, that I need to ask for forgiveness from?

_____

_____

What steps can I take to make amends or show that I am changing?

_____

_____

_____

Bonus

Write An Affirming Love Letter To Yourself

Take a few moments to slow down and reflect on how far you've come. This work—especially around healing, letting go, and forgiveness—is not easy. It asks you to meet yourself with honesty, compassion, and patience. That in itself is courageous.

Use this space to write a love letter to yourself as if you were writing to your dearest, most beloved friend—the one you'd never judge, the one you believe in wholeheartedly. Acknowledge your effort, your growth, and the intention behind the path you're walking. Even if you're still in the middle of it, you are showing up—and that matters deeply.

Here is an example of an affirming love letter centered around your forgiveness journey:

Dear [Your Name],

I see you. I see the quiet strength it takes to face the places inside that still ache. I see the way you keep showing up, even when the weight of the past feels heavy. I know this journey of forgiveness hasn't been easy—especially the forgiveness you're learning to offer yourself. But you're doing it. Gently. Bravely. At your own pace.

You are not weak for having been hurt. You are not broken because healing takes time. What you're doing now—choosing to look within instead of away—is an act of love. A radical, tender act of reclaiming your peace.

Thank you for showing up for yourself today—and every day. Even when it's difficult, even when the path feels unclear, you keep choosing to try. That matters more than you know. Choosing yourself, your healing, and your peace is not always easy, but it is brave. And I see your courage, even in the quiet moments.

You are doing hard, meaningful work—growing, unlearning, and showing up in new ways. You may not always feel strong, but the truth is: your willingness to keep going is strength. You are not behind. You are not broken. You are becoming.

You are worthy of the life you dream of—not someday, but now. Worthy of love that doesn't require you to shrink. Worthy of rest, of joy, of feeling at home in your own skin. You don't need to earn it by being perfect. You already are enough.

So I promise to keep walking with you, without judgment or harsh expectations. I will give you grace when you fall and encouragement when you rise. I will remind you of your worth when you forget. And I will always choose you over fear, over doubt, over old stories that no longer serve.

I love you deeply, completely, and without condition. Keep going. You are doing beautifully.

With love and gratitude,
[Your Name]

Chapter 8

Barrier:
Boundaries

Boundaries help us keep the good in and the bad out.
Setting boundaries inevitably involves
taking responsibility for your choices.
DR. HENRY CLOUD

Many of us were never taught what healthy boundaries look like, let alone how to set them. We may have been conditioned to believe that saying "no" is selfish, that putting our needs first is wrong, or that love requires self-sacrifice. However, the truth is that boundaries are not walls to keep people out—they are bridges that connect us more honestly and respectfully to ourselves and others. Boundaries are the invisible lines that protect our emotional well-being, define our values, and honor our capacity. Learning to set and uphold them is not about control or disconnection—it's about clarity, self-respect, and creating relationships where we can truly thrive.

Recognition Of The Barrier

A year after I met my then-boyfriend Rick, I started seeing a therapist. Things were getting serious with him, so I thought it would be best to talk to someone about it. I didn't really know what I was doing because this was technically my first real relationship.

Rick was eight years older than I, newly divorced with a son. I fell hard for him and didn't want to mess this up. I shared with her that I needed to address some things that I couldn't talk to anyone else about. She was the first person I was fully vulnerable with. I had no problems telling her everything because she legally couldn't share my business. I needed that one safe person with whom I could let myself be seen without judgment or worry that they would tell someone my private information.

She and I built a beautiful rapport. It wasn't long into our weekly sessions that she introduced me to this concept of boundaries. She recommended that I read the book *Boundaries* by Dr. Henry Cloud.[40] She showed great concern for my lack of boundaries based on what I shared with her about my life.

At the time I was a people pleaser, over-giver, and oversharer. The only real boundary I had was keeping myself from getting distracted by men. That boundary was set around twelve years old. My goals were to go to college, have a great career, buy a home, get married, have children, and travel. To ensure that I gave myself a fighting chance I stayed away from the distraction of boys until it was time. Sure, I had crushes, but that's about as far as it got for me in most cases. So I kept all men, until Rick, at a football field's distance away.

After several months of discussing my life and boundaries with my therapist, my newfound insight and practicing this concept called boundaries inspired me. I couldn't wait to tell one of my closest friends. She was like a big sister to me. At the time she was in medical school studying to become a psychiatrist. I shared with her all the ways in which I was going to start setting boundaries with people. I professed that for once, I was going to consider myself first. In true fashion, she was encouraging and happy as we talked about what I learned.

Later that day, she asked me to do something for her that I didn't want to do. I said, "No." With the look of shock on her face, without skipping a beat, she said, "I want you to put up boundaries with everyone except me." We laughed because that was a very real moment for both of us. Thankfully, we worked through it with no issues.

As I started to flex my boundary muscles, some people were not all that pleased with this new change. It was then that I realized that setting boundaries was going to be harder than I thought.

Getting comfortable with saying "no" was hard for me. I had to learn how to sit in the uncomfortable seat of disappointing others or letting them walk away while I held firm to my boundaries. Connection with others is meaningful to me, so it's not easy when others walk away. As a recovering people pleaser, I still don't like disappointing people. As a recovering over-giver, holding back on what I can offer presents a challenge at times.

When I was in my over-giving and other-focused stage of life, I rarely asked for much, if anything, from others. It's no wonder I attracted some pretty self-centered people into my life. These days, they may be classified as narcissists. In any case, to be on the receiving end of their disappointment was no fun.

My former therapist often reminded me that boundaries keep everyone safe. And they create a healthy balance in relationships.

Before I learned how to set healthy boundaries, I put up walls as a protective mechanism. The walls I created were out of fear and insecurities.

They allowed me to detach emotionally, whereas boundaries offer respectful limitations that still allow connection and interaction to occur.

Healthy boundaries allow you to give others a chance to understand how you wish to be treated. What I did previously was cut people out of my life and create an insurmountable wall without even considering any further interactions between us.

Setting boundaries has played a crucial role in fostering healthy relationships with others. Boundaries taught me how to take better care of myself. They also provided me with opportunities for growth in areas such as self-respect, consideration, and honesty.

> Boundaries keep everyone safe. And they create a healthy balance in relationships.

Understanding Boundaries

Learning about boundaries has been a journey of self-awareness and growth for me. At first, I didn't fully grasp what boundaries were or why they were so important. I often found myself people-pleasing or overextending myself, thinking that saying "yes" to everything would make others happy or strengthen relationships. However, over time, I started to notice that I was feeling drained, overwhelmed, and even resentful. I realized I was neglecting my own needs and not honoring my own limits, which affected my mental and emotional well-being.

Through reflection and experience, I began to understand that boundaries are not about being rigid or distant, but about respecting myself and my needs while still fostering healthy connections with others. I learned that it's OK to say "no" when something doesn't align with my values or when

I need time for self-care. I also realized that setting boundaries is an act of self-respect and an invitation for others to respect me in return.

As I practiced setting clearer boundaries, I noticed that not only did I feel more confident and at peace, but my relationships became more honest and balanced. Understanding boundaries has allowed me to protect my energy, prioritize my well-being, and engage more authentically with those around me.

Setting healthy boundaries is essential for maintaining my emotional, mental, and physical well-being. Without clear boundaries, I was risking overcommitting myself, neglecting my own needs, and becoming overwhelmed or resentful. Healthy boundaries helped me understand where my responsibilities and needs end, and where those of others begin, allowing me to preserve my sense of self and personal integrity.

Boundaries gave me a chance to prioritize self-care. Boundaries also allowed me to protect my energy from being drained by unhealthy dynamics. They empowered me to engage in relationships that are balanced, respectful, and fulfilling, while also maintaining the inner peace and clarity I need to navigate life's challenges.

Unhealthy Patterns Of Behavior With A Lack Of Boundaries

After reading Dr. Cloud's book on boundaries many years ago, I realized I needed to conduct further research to gain a deeper understanding of the unhealthy patterns of behavior that arise from a lack of boundaries.

We Become People Pleasers

There is a fear of disappointing others when we people please. We tend to neglect our own needs and desires in order to tend to others. It can be based on the fear of rejection as well.

We Tend To Overgive

We tend to overextend ourselves, thinking it shows loyalty and commitment. We take on responsibilities that aren't ours to take and find justification for it if challenged as to why we are overextending ourselves. We tend to live in a constant state of exhaustion.

Resentment Builds

We will sacrifice ourselves to meet others' wants, needs, and desires, later realizing that we aren't getting ours met. This leads to resentment and frustration in the relationship, which can be damaging.

We Have Difficulty Saying "No"

Saying "yes" even when we are overwhelmed and tired is a tough pattern to change, especially if you tend to be an over-giver or people pleaser.. There is a belief that we are not supposed to say "no" to others. We feel bad about it and guilty because we don't want to be perceived as selfish.

We Lack Self-Care

When we are focused on others, our self-care falls by the wayside. We put everyone before ourselves and find that we have very little time, if any, to care for ourselves.

We Feel Taken Advantage Of

There are people who will take advantage of our willingness to be helpful and will allow us to give without reciprocity. At times, they won't even appreciate what we've done, will want more, or play it off like it wasn't a big deal. This can make us feel exploited.

New Patterns Of Behavior To Create Healthy Boundaries

Creating healthy boundaries can feel intimidating, especially if you've spent much of your life silencing your own needs to keep the peace, avoid conflict, or earn approval. When you've been conditioned to put others first, setting limits can feel unfamiliar, even wrong. But the absence of boundaries doesn't make you more loving or loyal—it often leads to exhaustion, resentment, and disconnection from who you truly are. If you've struggled to speak up, say no, or protect your emotional space, know this: you are not alone, and you are not broken. You are learning something new. You are reclaiming your right to take up space, to protect your energy, and to trust what feels right for you. Boundaries aren't walls, they are acts of self-respect that build deeper trust within yourself.

Build Your Self-Confidence

One of the ways you can build your self-confidence muscle is by learning to be assertive. Focus on your values, needs, desires, and wants.

Maintain a healthy sense of self-respect, all while still respecting others. There is a balance between being considerate of others and honoring your own limits.

Practice More Self-Care

Preserving your energy requires you to nurture yourself, prioritizing your needs and desires. When you set boundaries you are ensuring that you are not depleting yourself. It's also a safeguard for your emotional, mental, and physical well-being.

Prioritize Your Well-Being

Self-empowerment is about taking responsibility for your happiness and well-being first and foremost. When you start to recognize and embrace your worth, it enables you to make choices that align with your values and desires. You can take your focus off everyone else and let go of resentment.

Respect Yourself

Every time you say "yes" to someone else when you really don't want to, you deny yourself. Your self-esteem takes another hit.

Honoring yourself by saying "no" is how you start to build self-respect. Be kind to yourself and learn how to say "no."

Practice Self-Preservation

Author and professor Audre Lorde wisely shares, "Caring for myself is not self-indulgence, it is self-preservation and that is an act of political warfare."[41] The practice of self-care is more than just having me time, it's a way of life. Practicing taking care of yourself daily is necessary.

Establish Boundaries

Establishing clear limits and communicating them effectively and ensuring that others respect your time, energy, and resources is how you assert your boundaries. This means you will have to express your needs, stand up for yourself, and protect your well-being.

Boundaries And Others

Boundaries are a two-way street. We must respect others' boundaries. We can't set an expectation that our boundaries be honored and not do the same. Honoring the boundaries of others is a gesture of goodwill: it's kind, respectful, and loving.

Learning to be with others and create healthy boundaries requires us to be better listeners. We have to be willing to ask questions in order to be clear about what the other person is sharing. We need to be able to tolerate being told "no" without punishing the other person or withholding from them because we didn't get our way.

We also need to respect other people's boundaries without making it about us and what we need. It can damage relationships when we want everyone to center us in their lives. You are the main character in your own story, no one else's.

We all have a right to give ourselves what we need and want. We have a right to protect ourselves, to privacy, and to respect. Having a community of people that can honor each other's boundaries creates a trust that can deepen the relationships. It's like saying to someone, "I see you, I hear you, and I respect you."

> You are the main character in your own story,
> no one else's.

You are free to take care of yourself the way you need to. That is what freedom looks like in a relationship with others.

Encouragement

To continue to open yourself up emotionally to an abusive or
addicted person without seeing true change is foolish.
Forgive, but guard your heart until you see sustained change.
DR. HENRY CLOUD

Oh, for the love of boundaries, allow yourself to let go of abusive relationships with people who don't respect you or your boundaries. This is a major act of self-love. There are professionals who can help you. Remember, boundaries can keep everyone safe both mentally and physically. Take some time to explore how healthy you are in the boundary department.

LoveWork—Your Opportunity

Here's your chance to work on your boundaries.

Get Your Healthy Boundaries On

Take your time and answer the following questions.

How could honoring and respecting your own and others' boundaries enrich your life?

_____

_____

_____

Are there people in your life who you allow to continue to step over your boundaries? If so, who?

_____

_____

_____

What boundaries are they crossing?

_____

_____

_____

Why do you believe you have been allowing this to happen?

_____

_____

_____

What do you need to do differently now with these people?

_____

_____

_____

Bonus

Let's be honest, most of us don't like boundaries when they're placed on us, especially when we're not getting our way. But here's the truth: Boundaries placed on us keep us safe too.

They invite us to grow, reflect, and relate more consciously. So if you're ready to evolve your relationships and expand your emotional maturity, try this bonus exercise.

Do you have a habit of crossing the boundaries others have set up? If so, why?

_____

_____

_____

_____

If you are challenged by this practice and need support, please reach out to a trusted therapist or coach who can support you.

Chapter 9

Barrier:
Fear

Understanding all the ways fear stands in the way
of our knowing love challenges us. Fearful that believing in
love's truths and letting them guide our lives
will lead to further betrayal, we hold back from love
when our hearts are full of belonging.

BELL HOOKS

---

o you remember the first time your heart broke? Most of us think of a romantic experience that broke our hearts, but in many cases our first heartbreak wasn't that. It could have been the first time you were yelled at by a caregiver. Or one of your parents promised to visit you but didn't. Perhaps it was the school bully who taunted you. It could have been hearing your parents fight as you listened from another room.

Recognition Of The Barrier

Once I experienced my first heartbreak it changed me. In the preface of her book, *All About Love*, bell hooks shared this passage:

> At the moment of my birth, I was looked upon with loving kindness, cherished and made to feel wanted on this earth and in my home. To this day I can't remember when that feeling of being loved left me. I just know that one day I was no longer precious . . .. The absence of their recognition and regard pierced my heart and left me with a feeling of brokenness so profound I was spellbound.[42]

At some level, I felt I could relate to that passage. What I know is that I never wanted to experience the pain of heartbreak again. I feared that I would not be able to withstand another blow to my heart. Regardless of the fear, I did experience heartbreak many more times with family and friends, and I broke my own heart.

There was a gene that God didn't give me. It was the Teflon gene. You know it: Even when someone hurts your feelings it doesn't hurt your heart and you can move past the hurt easily. It amazed me how others are able to not even be fazed by heartbreaking situations.

And then there's me. I need time to recover when my feelings have been hurt before I move forward. I remember a friend once told me that I needed to get my feelings hurt more often because of my level of sensitivity. She felt like I was taking too long to "get over it." But that's the thing: I can't get over it, I have to get through it.

Although I don't have that Teflon gene, I did create my own armor. I harnessed enough courage to try my hand at loving others again but each time things didn't turn out well, I added to my armor. The armor was the Charmaine-made Teflon to shield me from the anticipated blows that would come my way.

My armor was created because I was afraid. I feared being too exposed and what that could do to me. As much of a love bug as I am, I had a big fear of love. I was afraid that love won't love me back, and it would break me to the point of no return. So I allowed others in, but they couldn't get too close because my armor—fear—wouldn't let them. I did put down my armor a few times and got punched hard.

Facing the barrier of fear felt like someone asking me to hike Angels Landing at Zion National Park in Utah without any preparation. Although I enjoy hiking, that level of hiking requires preparation. I would need a coach to help me get my body ready for that hike. I'd want a person with experience to join me on the hike. I'd need to understand the route before I started. I'd need to know what to expect along the way and what hiking gear is needed for the journey. That's how I worked with the barrier of fear.

It didn't dawn on me that the very thing I was intrigued by and motivated by was the very thing that I was also afraid of. It was a double-edged sword. I feared being loved and that very love leaving me, again. And I feared that I would never truly experience real love.

It didn't help that the recurring messages I was hearing from others were: "Love is hard and it hurts," "you have to expect to be hurt," "those closest to you hurt you the most," and "trust no one ever."

Some of what I experienced or witnessed was that people give you their love and then take it back whenever they want. It was used as a way to control others. You would have to abandon yourself to gain the love of another, only to be hurt by it again. Love was used as an excuse for abuse (i.e., "I lost control because I love so much").

If this is what love is, why would we ever want it? It doesn't seem like a sustainable way to live. I desire relationships that are kind, trusting, and life-giving.

Rick was the exception; I didn't think I had much fear when it came to loving him freely. I was all in with him. His sustained actions early on in our relationship felt safe, kind, and real. It felt close to what I believed my grandmother had with my grandfather. We both were just easy together for a long time.

I couldn't believe I had found a sweet love like this. Yet, there was a lingering feeling of ending up alone. I feared him leaving me because of death, but not in life. When I think back to how long we were able to sustain our love, I feel blessed to have known that kind of love in my lifetime.

Understanding Fear

My past experiences, insecurities, societal conditioning, and the natural human tendency to want to protect myself from potential pain or vulnerability are the main reasons why I feared love. Overcoming this fear involved healing from past wounds, building my self-worth, and learning to embrace the uncertainty and beauty of emotional connection.

Unhealthy Patterns Of Behavior When Fear Is Present

Fear is a powerful emotion—it's meant to protect us, but when left unchecked, it often begins to control us. When fear is present, especially in relationships or personal growth, it can quietly shape our thoughts, decisions, and behaviors in ways that keep us stuck. Here's what I discovered through research and reflection: Fear doesn't just freeze us—it distorts us. It can lead us to self-sabotage, avoid vulnerability, or cling to control. Fear may convince us to stay silent when we need to speak up, to over-accommodate when we need to set boundaries, or to isolate ourselves when what we truly crave is connection. Many of these patterns become so normalized that we don't even recognize them as fear-based. But once we name them, we can begin to loosen their grip. In the following section, we'll explore some of the most common ways fear shows up in our behavior—and how we can begin to choose differently, from a place of courage and self-trust.

We Avoid Vulnerability

Exposing our true selves to someone else is risky business, especially when we have experienced being hurt or rejected before.

We Create Emotional Distance

We may create distance emotionally by keeping our feelings hidden. We tend to avoid genuine connection and intimacy when we notice things starting to get serious. Emotional distance is a way of playing it safe.

We Have Difficulty Trusting Others

Fear of love often results in a lack of trust in others. Those who fear being hurt or rejected may have trouble trusting that their partner will be there for them or will treat them with care and respect.

We Tend To Be Super Self-Sufficient

Some individuals may overemphasize their need for independence as a defense mechanism. We tend to push away support from others or refuse to rely on anyone emotionally. While it's healthy to maintain independence, extreme independence can be a way of avoiding the vulnerability and potential dependency that comes with love.

We Become Emotionally Unavailable

Emotional unavailability is another common pattern for people who fear love. Some may appear aloof, distant, or uninterested in deepening the emotional connection. They might keep conversations shallow or avoid engaging in vulnerable conversations, which makes it hard to build a strong emotional bond with others.

> Some individuals may overemphasize their need for independence as a defense mechanism.

We Tend To Play It Safe

Someone who fears love may avoid relationships altogether or only engage in superficial ones where there is little risk of emotional depth. They might stay in casual, short-term relationships or avoid commitment entirely to shield themselves from the vulnerability that comes with deeper emotional intimacy.

We Create Anxious Or Avoidant Attachments With Others

People who fear love might engage in a push-pull dynamic, where they vacillate between pulling someone close and pushing them away. They may seem interested and emotionally engaged at times, but then suddenly withdraw or shut down when the relationship deepens. This back-and-forth behavior creates confusion and uncertainty in relationships.

New Healthy Patterns Of Behavior When Fear Shows Up

Forming healthy patterns isn't about being fearless—it's about honoring ourselves, even when fear is present. That's where real growth begins. When we start to recognize fear and choose differently, something within us shifts. We move from reacting out of panic or self-protection to responding with self-awareness and trust. We speak our truth instead of staying silent. We set boundaries instead of bending ourselves to please others. We begin to show up more fully and honestly—even when it feels uncomfortable—because we're learning that our peace is worth protecting.

Embrace Vulnerability

Practice gradual openness. Instead of keeping your feelings hidden or retreating into emotional safety, start by sharing small, authentic parts of yourself with someone you trust. Vulnerability isn't a weakness at all; it strengthens and deepens connections and allows for authentic love.

Practice gradual openness. Instead of keeping your feelings hidden or retreating into emotional safety, start by sharing small, authentic parts of yourself with someone you trust.

Practice Being Emotionally Available

Practice engaging and being curious about your emotions. Instead of withdrawing when things get serious, be present with your feelings, giving yourself a chance to be with your feelings.

Learn Ways To Rebuild Trust

Begin by practicing gradual trust-building. Start with small, consistent acts of trust.

Trust is built over time. It's not about perfection but about the consistency of behavior. When others show up for you, acknowledge that and allow yourself to relax into the process.

Balance Independence And Interdependence

Embrace interdependence, where both individuals support and nurture each other's needs while also growing together. This means being able to ask for help or lean on someone emotionally when you need it, but also recognizing the value of giving and receiving support in a balanced way.

Regularly assess where you might be overly self-reliant. Are there times when you could benefit from letting others support you or show care? Ask for help when needed, whether emotionally or practically, and recognize that it does not diminish your independence; instead, it creates space for mutual growth.

Create Moments Of Connection

Start by allowing yourself to be present in the moment with others, even if that means experiencing discomfort. Engage in deeper conversations where you share not just surface-level details but your true emotions, thoughts, and desires. Create intentional moments of connection, whether through quality time, deep conversations, or physical affection.

Practice Deepening Relationships With Others

Seek out meaningful connections that allow for growth and deeper emotional exchanges. While it may feel scary to open up fully, commit to being present and engaged in relationships that encourage vulnerability, even if they come with challenges.

Take gradual steps toward deeper commitment, whether it's being emotionally available, engaging in more intimate conversations, or expressing affection. Choose not to settle for surface-level connections and instead seek out relationships that foster genuine growth.

Practice Consistency And Clarity

Instead of vacillating between pulling someone close and pushing them away, focus on clarity and consistency. Be mindful of your behavior, especially when it comes to emotional closeness. Communicate openly with those close to you about your feelings and needs, and commit to a steadier approach to the relationship.

When you feel the urge to withdraw, pause and reflect on the underlying reasons. Are you feeling scared or vulnerable? Practice expressing those fears rather than acting on them impulsively. Acknowledge your feelings and engage with them honestly instead of retreating.

Build Emotional Resilience

Recognize that love may sometimes bring challenges, but those challenges can be opportunities for growth. Work on building emotional resilience, so that when difficulties arise, you feel equipped to handle them without retreating.

Take time for self-reflection and emotional processing. Journaling, therapy, or talking with a trusted friend can help you navigate difficult emotions and stay connected to your authentic self during times of emotional vulnerability.

Fear And Others

All of your thoughts and feelings will be affected by your fears.
MICHAEL A. SINGER

The Harvard Study of Adult Development conducted an eighty-year study, the longest ever conducted on human happiness. It revealed, "The #1 insight from the Harvard study is that close relationships and social connections are crucial for our well-being as we age."[43]

Fear can profoundly affect the overall health of a relationship; finding ways to work through our fears for our well-being seems worth it. We run the risk of strained relationships when we live in constant fear. We don't need to address all our fears all at once. We address them as situations come up.

We all have a certain level of fear in our lives. Fear can be a powerful and pervasive emotion in relationships, often manifesting as a deep-seated anxiety about rejection, abandonment, or judgment from others. Our fears stem from past experiences, societal pressures, or internalized beliefs about our worthiness.

When we allow fear to dominate our interactions, it can lead to defensive behaviors, strained communication, and a reluctance to form genuine connections.

However, acknowledging and confronting these fears can be transformative. By embracing vulnerability and openness, we can build stronger, more authentic relationships where trust and understanding flourish.

Ultimately, facing our fears in the context of relationships can lead to personal growth and a deeper sense of connection with others.

Many individuals grapple with a variety of fears that can significantly affect their relationships. One of the most profound is the fear of abandonment, which stems from anxiety about losing a partner or being left behind, often rooted in past experiences or attachment issues.

Coupled with this is the fear of not having one's needs met, leading to feelings of isolation and dissatisfaction. Additionally, the fear of not being good enough can create self-doubt and insecurity, while the fear of rejection may result in defensive behaviors and reluctance to fully open up.

Conflict can also be a source of anxiety, as many worry that disagreements will hinder intimacy and communication. Furthermore, some individuals fear losing their freedom or autonomy in a relationship, while others carry the weight of past emotional pain that makes them hesitant to engage fully. Lastly, the fear of being found out—of being judged or rejected for one's true self—can prevent genuine connections from forming.

Addressing these fears is crucial for fostering deeper, more meaningful relationships.

Encouragement

It's important to create a safe and supportive community where you feel comfortable sharing your fears.

Start by being willing to acknowledge your fears to yourself. It is normal to have fears, and if we are able to address them in a healthy manner, it becomes a part of our personal growth.

Facing our fears is one of the bravest things we could ever do. What can happen is an increase in confidence, greater freedom, personal growth, and healthier interactions with others.

loveWork—Your Opportunity

Love is what we were born with. Fear is what we learned here.
MARIANNE WILLIAMSON

Seeking support from a trusted therapist or coach to work through your fears is a great strategy.

Take some time to journal about what has come up for you after reading this chapter on fear. Can you see some ways in which fear controls your relationships? If so, what are they?

_____

_____

_____

Bonus

Over the next week, pay attention to any fears that come up. Each night reflect and journal about your fears.

_____

_____

_____

_____

_____

_____

_____

_____

_____

_____

_____

_____

Chapter 10

Barrier: Comparison

The foundation for the barrier of comparison is laid for all of us at a very early age. From the moment we begin to interact with the world, we're taught—often subtly—that our worth is measured against others. Whether it's grades in school, appearance, achievements, or even the way we express emotions, we're shown that there is a "better" way to be—and that someone else is already doing it. Over time, this conditioning plants the belief that we're not enough as we are. We begin to look outward for validation and inward with judgment.

Comparison quietly becomes a lens we see ourselves through. It breeds self-doubt, resentment, and shame. It tells us our path should look like someone else's, that our pace is too slow, our voice too quiet, our wins too small. But comparison is not truth—it's distortion. It keeps us chasing someone else's life instead of honoring our own.

Recognition Of The Barrier

I used to work at a daycare center where I watched children from infancy through fifth grade. At the toddler age, I started to notice that they would cry and fight over who had the bigger toy. By the time they were at preschool age, they were watching for who looked like they had more

Goldfish crackers on their plate. When they reached elementary school, it was comparing height and wanting to be first at everything: first in line, first in the race, and so on.

Comparisons get more complicated as we get older. There was no way comparison was not a barrier on my path, but I didn't think about it because it was subtle. Although I had been working on loving myself well, I somehow still had a tendency to compare myself. I was trying to measure up when it came to achievements, looks, and career.

But who was I trying to match or exceed? There wasn't just one person; it was just a part of my life.

I wasn't aware of what I was doing until I watched a video from Louise Hay where she explained that comparison is damaging to all of us.[44] That's when I started paying attention to my thoughts and reactions when others had success. Sure enough, I would have thoughts like, "I should be in better shape," or, "I should be further along in my career like that person."

It was time to address this.

Understanding Comparison

We live in a world that constantly invites us to measure ourselves against others—be it their achievements, their looks, their success, or even their relationships.

While this external pressure is prevalent, the most insidious comparison often comes from within.

When we compare ourselves to others in relationships, it breeds feelings of inadequacy, insecurity, and disconnection. Rather than focusing on the uniqueness of our own experiences and connections, we fixate on what someone else has that we think we lack.

In relationships, this is especially dangerous because it distracts us from appreciating what we already have and who we already are.

The effects of comparison are not always obvious at first. It may begin with small thoughts like, "Their life looks so perfect compared to mine," or, "Why can't I be more like that couple who always seems to have it together?" But over time, these comparisons can undermine our self-esteem and even erode the bonds we share with the people we care about.

Instead of nurturing and growing together, comparison makes us look outward, creating a barrier between what is truly ours and what we perceive others have. What we fail to realize is that these comparisons often ignore the complexities of each relationship, ignoring the struggles, the compromises, and the effort that goes into making those connections work.

Unhealthy Patterns Of Behavior When Comparison Is Present

When comparison takes hold, it often leads us into subtle but destructive patterns. We begin to diminish our sense of worth or someone else's. We dismiss our strengths and overvalue what others have or appear to be. We might overwork ourselves to "catch up," downplay our accomplishments, or fall into cycles of jealousy and self-criticism. Social media, perfectionism, and the pressure to "keep up" only intensify these behaviors. Over time, comparison robs us of joy, gratitude, and the ability to see our lives clearly.

We Doubt Ourselves And Become Insecure

Constantly comparing ourselves to others can leave us feeling like we're not good enough, whether it's because we don't measure up to the "perfect" relationships we see online, or because we feel our partner isn't as attentive or affectionate as someone else's.

This self-doubt can make us second-guess our worth, leading us to place unhealthy pressure on ourselves and our partners. We start to wonder if we're doing enough, giving enough, or loving enough.

Over time, this erodes our sense of self and the authenticity of our connections.

We Develop Resentment And Jealousy

When we compare our relationships to those of others, we can fall into the trap of believing that others have it better, that they're getting something we're not. Perhaps it's more attention, more affection, or simply a partner or friend who seems to be "better" in some way.

This can easily turn into jealousy, where we begin to view our partner or friend as lacking or inferior. This feeling can destroy the trust and intimacy that a healthy relationship is built on, turning affection into competition. Rather than celebrating what makes our own relationships special, we focus on what they don't have in comparison to someone else's. Resentment starts to brew as we build expectations based on unrealistic comparisons.

We Experience Communication Breakdowns

We tend not to share how we honestly feel when comparison appears. We may start to distance ourselves emotionally from others, thinking, "What's the point? We're not like them."

Instead of having open, honest conversations about our needs, desires, or dissatisfaction, we retreat into silence, believing that we can't measure up or that the effort isn't worth it. This can lead to misunderstandings and feelings of isolation. Rather than working together, we drift apart, each of us harboring thoughts of what we *wish* the relationship looked like instead of focusing on the reality of what we have and how we can improve it together.

New Healthy Patterns Of Behavior For Comparison

The first step in breaking this cycle is noticing when we're measuring our worth by someone else's journey—and gently choosing to return to our own. This awareness is powerful. It allows us to pause, interrupt the inner narrative that says "you're not enough," and ask ourselves: Who am I without this comparison? What do I actually value? Returning to our own path doesn't mean ignoring others—it means honoring our own pace, our own needs, and our own growth. It's about shifting from competition to curiosity, from envy to inspiration.

Embrace Your Individuality

Honor your uniqueness and make space for the uniqueness of others.

Every person, every relationship is unique. Instead of comparing your relationships to others, try to focus on what makes your bond special. Celebrate the small moments, the quirks, and the depth that exists within your relationships.

Instead of questioning why your relationships don't look like someone else's, ask yourself what you value most about the connection you share. Reaffirm what you love and appreciate about each other, and understand that no one else's journey is yours to replicate.

> Every person, every relationship is unique. Instead of comparing your relationship to others, try to focus on what makes your bond special.

Practice Open, Authentic Communication

Instead of comparing and resenting, address any insecurities or concerns you may have in an honest way. Talk about what you need, and ask for what you want without fear of judgment.

Healthy communication invites vulnerability and trust, and when you allow yourself to be seen and heard in this way, the need to compare starts to fade.

When you express your feelings honestly, you open the door for others to do the same, creating a deeper bond that is based on mutual understanding rather than external validation.

Practice Gratitude

Take time to appreciate what you have rather than focusing on what you don't.

It can be easy to take your partner or your relationships for granted when you're constantly measuring it against others, but when you shift your focus to what's going well, you open the door to contentment.

The act of gratitude allows you to savor the unique qualities that make your relationship your own. Whether it's the way your partner looks at you, the way you laugh together, or the quiet moments you share, appreciating these can help to drown out the noise of comparison.

Support Your Individuality And Celebrate Your Successes As Well As Others'

Rather than seeing others' achievements as a reflection of your shortcomings, view them as inspirations towards your goals.

In a healthy relationship, growth is not a competition but a shared journey. Celebrate the success of others as much as your own, and work together to create a space where everyone can thrive.

In this environment, comparison fades away because each of you is focused on uplifting the other, not measuring against an external standard.

Comparison To Others

Comparison isn't just a barrier in romantic relationships—it can spill over into friendships, family dynamics, and even professional connections.

Comparing ourselves to others can create unnecessary competition. If we constantly measure our worth by how we stack up against others, we risk distancing ourselves from those we care about most.

Relationships thrive on mutual respect and support, not competition. Instead of comparing achievements or life stages, focus on celebrating each other's victories. Figuring out how to be genuinely happy for others allows relationships to flourish. There's space for all of us.

It's easy to fall into the trap of believing that someone else is doing things "better," which leads to strained relationships. We all have a unique rhythm, and what works for one may not work for another.

If you're constantly looking at the success of others, it can make you feel like your efforts aren't enough, even when you're doing your best. Instead, focus on your own growth and achievements, and be supportive of others' progress. Comparison can breed division and exclusion. True belonging comes from embracing who you are and finding a space where you are valued for your unique contributions and offering that to others as well.

Encouragement

I know it can feel overwhelming when you compare yourself to others, especially when it seems like everyone else has it all figured out.

But I want you to hear this: Your journey is *yours*—and it's so much more beautiful than any comparison could ever capture. You are not meant to follow someone else's path, to live to their standards, or to measure your worth against their achievements. What you've accomplished, how far you've come, and the person you're becoming are things only *you* can understand and appreciate.

I want you to take a moment and really see yourself—the progress you've made, the quiet strength you carry, the unique qualities that make you who you are. All of it matters.

You don't need to fit into anyone else's mold or live anyone else's story.

You are *enough*, right here, right now, just as you are. Don't let comparison steal your peace or your joy.

Embrace your own journey, with all its ups and downs, because it is *so* worthy of celebration. You are exactly where you're meant to be.

And that is something truly beautiful.

> Your journey is **yours**—and it's so much more beautiful than any comparison could ever capture. You are not meant to follow someone else's path, to live to their standards, or to measure your worth against their achievements. What you've accomplished, how far you've come, and the person you're becoming are things only **you** can understand and appreciate.

loveWork—Your Opportunity

Embrace Your Journey

Let's take a closer look at your journey.

What do you love most about your life?

_____

_____

_____

_____

What are you proud of accomplishing so far?

_____

_____

_____

_____

_____

Bonus

What are some words of encouragement you can say to yourself when you feel yourself comparing yourself to someone else? Write it here and in your journal. Below are a few examples.

"There is room for all of us. Someone else's light doesn't dim mine."

"Their journey is not my journey. I'm allowed to move at my own pace."

"I don't need to be like them to be worthy. I am enough as I am."

"I trust the timing of my life."

"My path is unfolding in its own beautiful way."

_____

_____

_____

_____

_____

_____

_____

_____

Chapter 11

Barrier:
Criticism

*To truly love ourselves, we must challenge our beliefs
that we need to be different or better.*

SHARON SALZBERG

*C*riticism can cut deep, especially when it comes from those we love, or when it echoes the harsh inner voice we've carried for years. For many of us, criticism doesn't feel like feedback; it feels like failure. It triggers shame, self-doubt, and a desperate urge to either defend ourselves or disappear. But not all criticism is the same, and not all of it deserves space in our hearts. In this chapter, we'll explore how to discern between harmful criticism and helpful reflection, how to soften the grip of our inner critic, and how to reclaim our voice when criticism has silenced us. The goal isn't to become immune to criticism, but to become rooted enough in self-worth that we no longer break under its weight.

Recognition Of The Barrier

One of my closest friends, her three daughters, and I were on our way out for a girls' day. The oldest of the girls said something negative about herself. It pained me to hear her talk about herself in a negative way. She is a beautiful young lady. With a smile, I looked at her and responded, "Hey, don't talk about my friend like that, she's wonderful just the way she is."

My goal was to affirm that she is enough, exactly as she is. But not even twenty-four hours later, I was criticizing myself in that same way. The irony, right? This was a sign that I needed to be mindful of all the ways in which I criticize myself.

As I worked on clearing my path so that love could freely exist, criticism appeared as a barrier, specifically destructive and negative criticism.

I spent a large portion of my life trying to avoid criticism from others. When we were young children, my cousins and I used to say, "Sticks and stones may break my bones, but words will never hurt me." But that wasn't true at all; at least for me, words did hurt my feelings.

In his book, *The Four Agreements*, Don Miguel Ruiz talks about how powerful our words are. He writes:

The word is not just a sound or a written symbol. The word is a force; it is the power you have to express and communicate, to think, and thereby to create the events in your life. You can speak. What other animal on the planet can speak? The word is the most powerful tool you have as a human; it is a tool of magic. But like a sword with two edges, your word can create the most beautiful dream, or your word can destroy everything around you. One edge is the misuse of the word, which creates a living hell. The other edge is the impeccability of the word, which will only create beauty, love, and heaven on earth. Depending upon how it is used, the word can set you free, or it can enslave you even more than you know. Your word is pure magic, and misuse of your word is black magic.[45]

I've reread this passage many times over the years as a reminder to myself. It was clear that I needed to clean up not only what I said about myself but also what I say to and about others. And, to include my thoughts.

Understanding Criticism

As within, so without, as above, so below,
as the universe, so the soul.
HERMETIC PHILOSOPHY

Where did all this criticism come from in the first place? There are several factors: our personal insecurities, being criticized by others, or as a defense mechanism.

My earliest memory of insecurity about my self-image started in fifth grade. I thought I was overweight, so the summer before starting middle school, I started dieting. I learned somewhere that eating one thousand calories a day would help me lose weight. So, I tried it.

I was in the kitchen making a tuna salad sandwich. My grandfather was observing me and looking quite perplexed. "What are you doing?" he asked me, probably because I was using mustard, with fewer calories, instead of mayonnaise to make my tuna salad.

I explained that I was on a diet and needed to lose weight. His countenance changed from perplexed to what I interpreted as concern and sadness.

"Mainey, you don't need to lose weight," he told me. But to my young mind, he didn't understand what I was going through. As nasty as that sandwich was, I ate it anyway.

For a long time after that, I was chasing this self-image that I thought would be more acceptable by the world's standards. I still catch myself at times now.

Criticism is basically an evaluation or judgment about shortcomings. When researching the effects of criticism, I came across many articles. One of the articles was written by therapist Andrea Hollingsworth. She writes, "As far as our brains are concerned, criticism, wherever it's coming from (even our own selves), feels like assault. So stress hormones like cortisol get pumped into our body, preparing us to fight, flee, freeze, or fawn." She further explains that research shows that a chronically activated threat-detection system can wreak havoc on both physical and emotional health.[46] This led me to explore the effects of criticism.

Overexposure to cortisol and other stress chemicals puts us at increased risk for:

- Anxiety and depression
- Memory and focus problems
- Weight gain
- Heart disease and stroke
- Headaches
- Digestive issues
- Sleep problems

I was familiar with experiencing the above effects of overexposure to cortisol and other stress chemicals. I certainly didn't like having anxiety, mild depression, an inability to fully focus, sleeping problems, or weight gain.

It was time to figure out how to move the barrier of criticism out of my way.

This was an inside job. Based on Hermetic philosophy, whatever is going on inside of me is reflected in my external world. Working with my inner critic seemed to be where I needed to start.

In moments of reflection, I noticed that not only was I critical of myself, but I created an existence where I was around people who were critical of me. I noticed that I didn't have a healthy sense of self-value, so I didn't have very many people in my life who valued me. I also became critical of others.

The first leg of the journey was to learn how to work with my inner critic. I needed to form a new relationship with her. My inner critic can be a mean girl. Even when something good happens, she will jump in quickly, whispering all kinds of negative things. "You're not good enough," "You're going to fail," and "No one really cares about or likes you."

Her favorite attack method is comparison. Sharon Salzberg addresses the inner critic quite beautifully in her book *Real Love*. "Mindfulness helps us see the addictive aspects of self-criticism—a repetitive cycle of flaying ourselves again and again, feeling the pain anew," Salzberg explains.[47]

Her insight also helped me understand that each time I judge myself harshly, I was reinforcing my sense of unworthiness.

> I created an existence where I was around people who were critical of me. I noticed that I didn't have a healthy sense of self-value, so I didn't have very many people in my life who valued me. I also became critical of others.

Shortly after studying the effects of the inner critic, I began to see how much this negativity affected my well-being, and not in a positive way. I had unconsciously identified with those negative remarks and they made a home in my body. It's no wonder that I had anxiety and high blood pressure.

Getting to the place in my life where what others say about me doesn't bother me, as well as working on my own criticism, took effort and time on my part. It was like a gym workout every day for a while. I remember watching the tide turn; it was turning toward self-love. Learning that the remarks of the inner critic are just thoughts unconnected to the reality of life helped me tremendously.

Another major stride I made in this area of criticism was regarding Salzberg's suggestion on dealing with my inner critic. She recommends not fighting with the inner critic but having a gentle approach with her. There are times I've gently reassured her by saying, "It's OK, I know you're trying to keep me safe, but everything is OK."

It's not that we can fully banish our inner critic, but with mindfulness practice, we are able to loosen its grip on us. This holds true for criticizing others.

Unhealthy Patterns Of Behavior With Criticism

Criticism, especially when it's constant, harsh, or unpredictable, can leave a deep and lasting imprint. Whether it comes from a parent, partner, teacher, or your own inner voice, repeated criticism begins to shape how you see yourself and how you move through the world. Over time, you may start second-guessing your decisions, silencing parts of who you are, or chasing perfection in hopes of avoiding judgment. These responses often start as protection—survival strategies designed to shield you from pain.

Here are some unhealthy patterns of behavior that form the barrier of criticism.

We Tend To Focus On What's Wrong

We tend to only focus on what's wrong. We tend to highlight the flaws or mistakes. We maintain a running narrative about a person or situation that is negative.

We Point Out Others' Character Instead Of Our Own

We criticize someone's character by placing our personal judgment on them. When we point out or criticize someone else's character, we're often projecting our own insecurities, fears, or unmet needs onto them. Instead of reflecting on our own behaviors, flaws, or biases, it can feel easier to focus on the perceived shortcomings of others.

We Make Comparisons

We compare someone else to others or compare ourselves to others. These practices make them—or ourselves—inferior or less; there tends to be some level of inadequacy involved.

We Tend To Be Judgmental

It can be demoralizing when we make judgements, or blame or shame others, especially in the presence of others.

We Make Everything About Us

If your feedback is more about venting your own frustration or dissatisfaction instead of addressing the other person's actions or needs, it's probably criticism.

We Use Negative Language

If your tone or choice of words feels dismissive, condescending, or harsh, it's a sign you may be criticizing someone. Phrases like "always," "never," or "why can't you," can sound judgmental or accusatory.

Healthy Patterns Of Behavior With Criticism

Forming healthy patterns of behavior when criticism is at play matters because it lifts the heavy weight of self-doubt and fear that often follows harsh judgment. When we learn to respond with self-compassion instead of self-attack, we build resilience and protect our sense of worth. These healthy habits help us see the difference between constructive feedback that encourages growth and destructive negativity that undermines us. This shift not only safeguards our emotional well-being but also empowers us to show up authentically and confidently—in our relationships, work, and life. Ultimately, nurturing a healthier relationship with criticism is a vital step toward greater peace and deep self-love.

Focus On What's Right

Instead of only pointing out flaws, highlight the strengths and positive aspects of the person or situation. Offer encouragement by focusing on what's working and how to build on it.

Acknowledge Actions, Not Character

Rather than criticizing someone's character, focus on their actions and behavior, separating their worth from their mistakes. Acknowledge what they've done and provide guidance on how to improve.

Respect Individuality

Instead of comparing, celebrate the uniqueness of each person. There is no need to compete with others. What others offer doesn't take away what you have to offer.

Practice Empathy

Rather than being judgmental, show empathy and understanding. Focus on providing support rather than placing blame, and aim to create a safe, healthy community where we all have a chance to grow.

Practice Being More Thoughtful

Instead of making it about your frustrations, center your feedback on the other person's needs and growth. Be thoughtful about how your words can help them improve, rather than simply venting your dissatisfaction. If your needs aren't getting met, please make sure you take care of getting your needs met as well.

Use Constructive Language

Replace negative or harsh language with positive, encouraging words. Aim to be kind and constructive, and avoid phrases that sound accusatory or dismissive.

> Rather than being judgmental, show empathy and understanding. Focus on providing support rather than placing blame, and aim to create a safe, healthy community where we all have a chance to grow.

Criticism And Others

Whatever happens around you, don't take it personally . . .
Nothing other people do is because of you.
It is because of themselves.
DON MIGUEL RUIZ

In the midst of writing this book, my best friend called me to tell me that her youngest child was being bullied in school. Her classmates were calling her ugly. My heart hurt for this little nugget that I love dearly. I was angry and sad for her.

We were all on FaceTime, so I immediately went into Aunt Charmaine mode. We talked about what happened. I told her how pretty, lovable, and smart she is. Her response was, "No, I'm not." She believed her classmates.

Some may say, "Oh, they're just being kids." Perhaps, but I now recognize the change in her. She's sensitive now when it comes to her looks. Our formative years matter. With our young minds, we make big meaning out of the things that happen to us. I'm well aware of that. She is one of my many reasons why I show up and do this every day. The legacy of love I want her to experience and carry on matters. Removing this barrier is in honor of the young people I get to be godmother and aunt to.

When dealing with criticism and others, Don Miguel Ruiz's teaching on his second agreement, "Don't Take Anything Personally," helps me navigate the times when criticism from others comes to my doorstep.

Easier said than done, I know. We all get so offended by others, don't we? I used to get caught up in their opinion of me, valuing it over what I know about myself. I would even make meaning of who I am based on what they said. Seeing this as a part of the barrier, I realized a practice of self-approval was in order.

Author Louise Hay is known for sharing her wisdom of self-love by encouraging us to love and approve of ourselves. Practicing self-love and self-approval also helped me love and accept others for who they are.

The barrier of criticism was crumbling daily. That space has opened up since the practice of appreciation has led me to a deeper love of myself and others.

Encouragement

Do what you feel in your heart to be right—
for you'll be criticized anyway.
You'll be damned if you do, and damned if you don't.
ELEANOR ROOSEVELT

It's time to open up to a greater love of yourself.

Don't deny the pleasure of love, acceptance, and approval for yourself. I'm not talking about being vain or arrogant. What I invite you to do is gently let go of all the negative thoughts you have about yourself and others. Practice talking to yourself like you would talk to the person you love the most, and if that doesn't help, talk to yourself the way you believe the god of your understanding would talk to you. If that doesn't work, talk to yourself like the most supportive coach or mentor would.

loveWork—Your Opportunity

I Love And Approve Of Myself Exercise

Fill this space by listing what you love and approve of about yourself. In the letter, include things you love about yourself—your achievements, personality traits, strengths, and things you are proud of. Visit this list often.

_____

_____

_____

_____

_____

_____

_____

_____

_____

_____

_____

_____

_____

_____

_____

_____

Bonus

The Critic Assessment

If one or both of these statements below apply to you, please complete the exercises below.

Statement: I often find myself criticizing others.

Opportunities for improvement: Discuss areas where growth is possible or adjustments can be made. (*Example: I will be more mindful of what I am saying about others.*)

_____

_____

_____

_____

_____

Suggestions for development: Offer specific, actionable steps to enhance performance. (*Example: I will not participate in gossiping about others and not center my conversations around other people's business.*)

_____

_____

_____

_____

_____

Statement: I often compare myself to others.

Opportunities for improvement: Discuss areas where growth is possible or adjustments can be made. (*Example: I will focus on my uniqueness, my value, and my worth.*)

_____

_____

_____

_____

_____

Suggestions for development: Offer specific, actionable steps to enhance performance. (*Example: I will spend time focusing on my personal growth.*)

_____

_____

_____

_____

_____

If you are challenged by this practice and need support, please reach out to a trusted therapist or coach who can support you.

Chapter 12

Barrier:
Approval

Don't be concerned about being disapproved of.
Be concerned about the consequences of avoiding disapproval.
ANTHONY DE MELLO

---

ncountering disapproval from others can be a tough pill to swallow. When I was criticized or excluded, heard dismissive comments, or was gossiped about, it made me feel like I was not measuring up or that I was not good enough. Sometimes, it's the sharp remarks that sting the most.

It was hard not to internalize those moments, especially when I felt like I was being judged or misunderstood.

But I've learned over time that while disapproval can hurt, it doesn't define my worth. Their disapproval often said more about their own expectations or values than it did about me. I understand that now.

Recognition Of The Barrier

Validation feels good, but not when you need it from everyone. There is no way you will win everyone's approval, ever. What matters most is staying true to myself and not letting others' opinions invalidate my self-worth.

It's important to discern whether feedback is constructive or if it's just someone else's reflection of their own discomfort, lack of knowledge, or biases. I can only do that by checking in with myself about my own truth. Rather than letting disapproval continue to knock me down, I've found it helps to focus on the positive relationships with the people who really know me.

> Validation feels good, but not when you need it from everyone. There is no way you will win everyone's approval, ever.

Anthony De Mello, author of the book *Awareness*, was the first teacher who shined a light for me on how damaging the need for approval from others is to our well-being. He calls the need for approval a drug. When we get praised, it gives us a high. If we are booed, it brings us down.

As someone who used to be on stage a lot, I get how it feels when others praise you for your talent; it feels great. You can get addicted to that feeling. But it's always that one person who doesn't think you're that great that sticks out the most.

I had someone once tell me that my voice was not as pretty as that of one of my fellow bandmates. His comment stung. I found myself practicing more and trying to sing more softly to win over his approval. Why did that one person's opinion matter so much? He didn't play any significant role in my life or singing career.

I started paying attention to how approval was showing up in my life—from how I behaved when wanting approval to the disappointment of not meeting someone else's approval and even how others behaved toward me when I didn't meet their approval standards.

Once I noticed it, it was exhausting. I wanted off the ride of approval. Depending on others' approval caused me unnecessary suffering.

According to De Mello, "You can truly love others when you don't need them emotionally."[48] I decided to test De Mello's theory to see if I could move the approval barrier out of the way. Stick with me here. I didn't understand this at first.

Understanding Needing Approval

What I now understand is that my need for approval was all based on fear. If others approved of me, they wouldn't leave me. I wouldn't feel the sting of rejection or being not enough. Fear controls a lot of our lives, and we are often unaware. It's what's underneath most of our pain points.

Before I started the removal process for this barrier, I journaled and read as much as I could about approval and healthy relationships. I put my attention on my behavior, and when I noticed I was "performing" to gain approval, acceptance, or validation.

Surrendering to the idea that I no longer needed to gain the approval of others to live in peace caused major shifts in my life. Relational changes started to happen. I noticed that as I began to actively approve of myself, it was easier to let go of the need for others' approval or disapproval. Once I saw it and the damage it did to my well-being, I couldn't unsee it. There was no going back, no matter who or what it was.

> As I began to actively approve of myself, it was easier to let go of the need for others' approval or disapproval.

Unhealthy Patterns Of Behavior When Needing Approval From Others

Let's look at the patterns that I found associated with this barrier. The innate human desire for social connection and acceptance is a fundamental aspect of psychological development. However, when the pursuit of external validation becomes a dominant driver of behavior, it can manifest as a series of unhealthy approval-seeking patterns. These patterns, characterized by a persistent need for praise and a fear of disapproval, often lead to a diminished sense of self, increased anxiety, and a compromised ability to form authentic relationships.

We Tend To Be People Pleasers

We can find people-pleasing as an unhealthy pattern of behavior across many of the barriers. We constantly go out of our way to make others happy, often at the expense of our own needs or desires. We tend to agree to things we don't want to do or suppress our true feelings just to gain approval.

We Tend To Be Overdependent On Others' Opinions

Our self-worth muscle needs to be worked on when this pattern appears. When we rely heavily on external validation and the opinions of others, it can damage our self-esteem. We often feel not good enough or a failure when someone doesn't approve of our actions.

Relying on compliments, feedback, or recognition from others to feel good about ourselves is also damaging to our self-worth. If we aren't careful, this leads to an unstable sense of identity.

We Suppress Our True Self

We tend to avoid speaking up or taking risks out of fear that others may not be pleased with our decisions. There's a fear of rejection or judgment. It doesn't allow us to form authentic connections.

We Become Perfectionists

Those who tend to be perfectionists overwork themselves, trying to meet the unrealistic expectations set by others and themselves. There's a belief that if they are flawless, they will win or keep the approval of others and themselves.

We Hide Who We Really Are

We tend to sacrifice ourselves by hiding parts of our personality, beliefs, or values when we think others won't accept them. We may pretend to be like someone else that we deem more likable or accepted.

New Healthy Patterns Of Behavior For Approval

Have you ever noticed how much your sense of worth can hinge on what others think or say? For many of us, seeking approval from friends, family, or colleagues becomes a lifelong habit, often causing us to overlook the most vital source of validation—ourselves. But self-approval is about more than just feeling good; it's about building a steady foundation of acceptance and kindness that stands strong, no matter what others say. In this section, we'll explore why cultivating healthy habits of self-approval is essential, not only for our emotional well-being but also for living with authenticity and confidence.

Embrace Self-Assertion

Standing up for your well-being by saying "no," creating boundaries or sharing your needs or desires—even if it disappoints or annoys others— takes courage for a recovering people pleaser. It garners self-respect and it displays that you understand that you deserve to be treated, cared for, and considered in the relationship as well.

Build Self-Worth From Within

Allowing and embracing your authentic self helps you build your self-worth muscle. Practice acknowledging who you are. Appreciate your uniqueness as a gift to the world.

Give yourself compassion, especially when things are hard.

Celebrate your moments of growth and expansion into your true self.

Cultivate Authenticity

Embracing who you truly are is such a loving gift to give to yourself. A daily practice of deep connection with yourself, like meditation or journaling, can help. When you are genuine, you tend to attract people who appreciate you for who you are. Healthy relationships are built on authenticity, not a facade.

Embrace Your Humanity And The Journey

Our journey is about progress, not perfection. We are going to make mistakes, we are not going always to make the best decisions, nor will we meet all of our goals.

When we drop the weight of perfectionism, we become lighter and freer. We can also foster healthier, more sustainable relationships.

Honor Your True Self

Living in alignment with your beliefs, values, and personality gives you a deep sense of contentment and inner peace. Allow yourself to come out of hiding for fear of judgment with an understanding that people may judge you, but that's not your business or your concern anymore.

Build Emotional Resilience

Now that you are aligning with your true self, accept that not everyone will agree with you or approve of you or what you are doing. Honoring yourself also comes with learning to handle rejection as an opportunity to grow in your self-worth. We are resilient, we are capable of dusting ourselves off and moving forward. Each time you do, you build your self-confidence, strength, and sense of worthiness.

Approval And Others

There was a significant moment not too long ago when I realized that I had made some big strides regarding approval. It was two years after Rick's death. An acquaintance and I reconnected; he was a friend of Rick's. He asked me with what seemed like concern about how I was doing, with an expectation in his voice of hearing that I'm not in a good place. I responded, "I'm good. I miss Rick so much. I hate how things ended with us, but I'm good."

He seemed appalled and almost offended by my acknowledgment that I was doing well.

"Charmaine, there is no way you are OK," he said. I assured him I was. I told him that if he had asked me a year ago, I would have told him something different.

"Well, there have been some really bad things said about you," he said. I assured him I no longer cared.

"You have to care what others think, Charmaine; everyone does."

I checked in with my feelings. I felt calm and at peace. I could sense he was confused and frustrated.

He didn't know how much time, attention, commitment, and dedication I'd put into my healing. My healing has set me free, and those around me are free as well. I felt at peace and free.

So let's return to Anthony De Mello's statement that I mentioned earlier in this chapter, "You can truly love others when you don't need them emotionally." This idea of emotional independence has been a game-changer for me. Emotional independence means I take responsibility for my own feelings and emotional well-being, without relying on anyone else to make me feel happy, worthy, or accepted. When I approach relationships from a place of emotional wholeness instead of neediness, my love comes from a much healthier, more authentic space.

When I'm not clinging to someone for emotional security or approval, I can focus on building a connection based on mutual respect, admiration, and authenticity, rather than trying to extract something I'm missing within myself.

Emotional independence allows me to let go of the unhealthy dynamics of codependency, where I might have relied too heavily on others for emotional fulfillment or approval. Now, I'm more able to maintain my own individuality and emotional balance, which makes it easier to create genuine, trust-filled relationships.

When I love without needing approval, I notice that my relationships feel more equal and fulfilling. Love becomes a conscious choice, not a transaction based on what I expect to get from someone.

I've found that the most authentic love doesn't come from wanting to fulfill my unmet emotional needs or seeking constant validation, but from a place of self-sufficiency, care, and acceptance of myself. I can now truly love others because I don't need them emotionally, nor do I need to seek their approval to feel validated, especially from those with whom I don't have a relationship.

I now know what it means to be in interdependent relationships, not codependent relationships.

One important thing to remember is that we can be fickle at times. We change our minds on a dime. I'm not sure we will ever be able to meet the approval of another person completely. Even if we do somehow, the needle gets moved, and the race through the approval cycle starts over again. It is a never-ending cycle of misery.

Letting others off the hook when it comes to meeting your approval allows real connection and happiness to occur with the relationship. We don't need other people's approval, nor do others need ours to live happily and free. Let's give each other the dignity and respect of our own life path.

Encouragement

Maybe you have it all together in the approval department, and if so, lucky you for not being affected by it. But for those of us who have suffered unconsciously because of the need for approval, I have good news. You don't have to continue to painfully participate in what Anthony De Mello calls the drug of approval. With practice, you will be able to free yourself from it. And when you slip back into the old pattern of behavior, you will know how to get back into alignment.

LoveWork–Your Opportunity

Embracing Self-Approval: Your Life Is Worth Enjoying

This exercise invites you to reflect on what truly matters to you and how embracing self-approval can help you live a fuller, happier life. Answer the questions below honestly, using them to uncover what brings you joy, what fears might be holding you back, and how you can begin to honor your own worth without relying on others' approval. This practice is about recognizing that your life is worth enjoying on your own terms.

Reflect on these questions:

What is most meaningful in life to you?

_____

_____

_____

What makes you genuinely happy?

_____

_____

_____

What are the things you want to do but hold back from because of the fear of judgment or criticism?

_____

_____

_____

Now that you understand the power of self-approval, are you willing to take steps toward doing what you've been afraid to try? If yes, what is one action you can take right now to honor yourself and your desires?

_____

_____

_____

_____

_____

Bonus

Reclaiming Your Approval

This bonus exercise is an invitation to pause and gently examine where you may still be seeking validation outside of yourself. By identifying whose approval you're chasing and how it's impacted your sense of self, you can begin to shift that energy inward, toward self-trust and self-respect. Take your time with each question, and let your answers come from a place of honesty and curiosity, not judgment.

Reflect on the following:

Whose approval am I trying to meet outside of my own?

_____

_____

How has their need for approval affected my sense of self-worth and value?

_____

_____

In what ways can I begin practicing self-approval today?

_____

_____

This reflection is about beginning the courageous work of choosing yourself, over and over again.

Epilogue

We have addressed some of the major barriers that hold us back from experiencing the fullness of love. I believe the journey continues for as long as we are living. You will discover that there are other barriers that appear on your personal journey. As you continue to work through these barriers and others, may you find the strength to keep going. May you enjoy the experience of love's embrace that has been here the whole time.

You can all thank the Disney movies of my childhood. They sparked this whimsical dream about life and my own happily ever after. Sure, there were fleeting thoughts that I could possibly face adversities like all the main characters. Even at a young age, I understood how the adversities they faced always turned out to be treasured lessons. Their triumphs spoke to the ability that they could get through tough and scary situations.

I was hoping to skip the adversity part in my own life. But I didn't get to skip it. Yet, that young girl that still lives inside me never stopped believing that one day I would have that magical dance like Princess Belle in *Beauty and the Beast* did as she danced into her happily ever after: a tale as old as time.

Perhaps this is my Disney story, titled *Charmaine*. Unlike Disney, though, this is real life. This is earth school, a quest nonetheless: the quest of self-discovery and personal growth. All of the "supporting characters"— no matter what role they played—led me to the greatest understanding of love so far. Every single experience, whether it was hardship or pure bliss, was a lesson of love.

Whether we realize it or not, spiritual leader Ram Dass reminds us that "we are all just walking each other home."[49]

Life is moving quickly; I feel like I was just playing in my grandma's front yard with my cousins. Because of the swiftness of time, I try to cherish as many moments as I can while I'm here. Harmon Okinyo said, "Time is a currency you can only spend once, so be careful how you spend it."[50]

While there will always be room for growth, we also have to enjoy life now. There are lots of unsettling things happening in our world. Maybe you are part of the world's story of happily ever after. The health of our world depends on how healthy we are individually. If we all make the choice to work on being the healthiest individual we can be relationally, mentally, and physically, we can help the world find its way to happily ever after.

I'm willing to try.

I hope you are, too.

This journey of self-discovery and personal growth isn't over for me. It won't be until I take my last breath on this earth. Yes, I've known both success and failure in the love arena. I proudly take my place with the rest of you who are also daring greatly by actually being in the arena too, and not just sitting in the cheap seats commenting about the rest of us. I am paying attention, and I'm in awe as I witness others bravely return to love after a major letdown. It inspires me to keep going.

I know love has so much more to show me. Wherever it takes me, I know that in the end, everything is OK.

As far as my happily ever after goes, I'm in it. I'm living life and love in real time. This is the real-life story of the human experience of Charmaine, a woman who bravely went on a quest to find true, meaningful connections.

It was always all about love.

Encouragement

Everything will be okay as soon as you are okay with everything. And that's the only time everything will be okay.
Michael A. Singer

Congratulations, You've made it through the entire book. My hope is that you are experiencing more inner peace and a greater sense of love for yourself and others. Thank you for showing up for yourself once again. You are a worthy cause.

I invite you to participate in this last opportunity for LoveWork—at least in this book.

I hope you are proud of all the ways you've allowed yourself to grow and expand. It's time to celebrate you!

LoveWork—Your Opportunity

Celebrations are such a sweet part of life. It's a great way to express self-love. Whether it's your own private ceremony or a celebration that you invite others to is up to you.

Below are some elements of setting up your celebration as your final LoveWork activity.

You are worth celebrating. Have fun. Cheers to you!

Acknowledge And Appreciate What You've Done

You are worth recognizing. Far too many times we put emphasis on what we aren't doing right and forget to celebrate and acknowledge all the ways we are getting on in life well. Upon completing an achievement, like getting through this book, it's nurturing to your well-being to honor yourself.

Have A Private Celebration, Or Invite Other People

Most of my celebrations are private fun. Inviting other people is also fun, and you get a feeling of support from your community. You can make it formal or casual. It creates a sense of shared happiness.

Create Expressions Of Gratitude

A life well lived is my "thank you, God." If you feel moved to, you could write a letter to the God of your understanding of how grateful you are.

When I have invited others, I get to thank them as well, which feels good to do. And please don't forget to thank yourself.

Plan How You Will Celebrate

Celebrations often incorporate rituals such as singing "Happy Birthday," gift-giving, or lighting candles. I like listening to music, dancing, cooking a great meal, and going out to dinner. There are times when I light a candle and say a prayer as well.

Nourish Yourself With Your Favorite Meal And Drink

Most celebrations involve food and drink. Preparing a delicious meal or treating yourself to a night out is a great way to satisfy all of your senses.

Buy Yourself A Symbolic Gift

Gifting is not one of my primary love languages; however, I will sometimes buy myself something that is symbolic of what I'm celebrating. You can have lots of fun with this. I've even bought myself cards.

Celebrate With Music And Entertainment

Music is my ultimate love language. Music brings in an element that creates whatever mood you want to be in. Music is always a part of my celebrations.

Take Some Time To Reflect

Journaling has become a way of life for me. I spend time reflecting on the significance of the celebration and what happened along the way.

Create An Experience

Create an experience by decorating your space that sets the mood for the celebration. This is a way to bring out your own creativity.

Capture The Moment

Taking photographs and videos is now a way of life for us. Creating keepsakes is also a way to capture the moment.

Bonus

I'd love to celebrate with you. If you are willing to share your love ceremony and celebration with me please do. Here's how you can share it.

Email: thecouragetorise@charmaineheard.com

Tag me on social media:

IG: @charmaineheard

FB: Charmaine Heard Consulting

Keep going!

Love always,
Charmaine

Don't ever think I fell for you, or fell over you.
I didn't fall in love, I rose in it.
TONI MORRISON

Acknowledgments

My late husband, Rick: I will forever be thankful for the love we shared. I'm sure if you are watching from the other side, you can see it all clearly now.

To my parents and the rest of my family: Your love was my foundation. Your support, care, and grace has carried me through more than I can ever fully express. Thank you for believing in me when I doubted myself, for showing up in quiet ways and loud ones, for cheering me on, and for holding space when I needed to pause. Whether through words, presence, prayers, or simple understanding, you've been my safe place, my reminder of where I come from. I'm so grateful for each of you. This journey has been made sweeter, stronger, and more meaningful because of your love. From the depths of my heart: thank you.

To all my friends: Thank you. Your love, support, and encouragement have meant more than words can say. I truly wanted to name each of you (and believe me, I tried!), but the list was simply too long, a beautiful reminder of how lucky I am to be surrounded by such incredible people. From the bottom of my heart, thank you.

Your presence, belief in me, and kindness have carried me through this journey in ways you may not even realize. And to those who encouraged me consistently along the way—you know who you are—your steady support made all the difference.

Honorable mentions to a few souls who went above and beyond, offering kind words, timely check-ins, thoughtful feedback, or simply holding space for me when I needed it most. You reminded me what true friendship looks like, and I'll never forget it: Tamu, Michael, David, Carey, Barbara, Jennifer, TC, Rob, Ayeesha, Gargi, Tasha, Rhonda, Alana, Adrienne, Arielle, Raven, Stephanie, Roxane, Teresa, Amar, Kathryn, Gail, Naïm, Bobette, Medaris, Carmen, Kathleen, Love at the Center crew, Leaders of Love crew, Shanda, The Almonds, and Von.

Special thanks to my mentors, coaches, and therapists who helped me along the way.

Thank you to the young people who know me as their godmom, "aunt" or simply Charmaine.

To my clients, past and present: You are all truly amazing human beings. It has been a pleasure and an honor to support you on your journey. Thank you.

To my dear friend Ann Lam-Anh Pham: Thank you from the depths of my heart for creating the cover that brought this book to life. Your artistry captured more than just an image—you captured its spirit. I was in awe the first time I saw it, and I still am. But it wasn't just your talent that moved me—it was your generosity, your belief in this project, and the love you poured into every detail. You gave this story a face, a voice, and a first impression I'm proud of. I'll never forget what a gift it was to have you by my side in this journey. Thank you for making this dream more beautiful than I ever imagined.

Dear Indie Books International Team and Bonnie: I want to extend my heartfelt thanks for your incredible support, professionalism, and dedication throughout this journey. Your belief in my work and your commitment to excellence have made this experience not only rewarding but deeply meaningful.

From editorial guidance to the care taken in production and design, your team's attention to detail have brought this project to life in a way I could only imagine. It has truly been a privilege to collaborate with such a talented and thoughtful group.

About The Author

Charmaine Heard is a highly credentialed international relationship intelligence coach. The essence of her work is about clarity, self-awareness, relational growth, and meaningful connection. She holds a bachelor of science degree in marketing and brings over twenty years of leadership experience, including roles as director of programs and vice president of operations at various organizations.

Charmaine is deeply passionate about fostering healthy leadership and believes that cultivating strong interpersonal skills is essential for leaders, enabling organizations to thrive.

Charmaine also has extensive experience managing corporate and private educational programs for adult learners, leveraging this background to deliver impactful leadership and professional development training to organizations.

In addition to her coaching, Charmaine facilitates workshops and offers both one-on-one and group coaching. She has led educational programs in schools, universities, and both nonprofit and for-profit organizations, always focused on creating positive, healthy, and flourishing environments.

Works Cited And Author's Notes

1 Mari Perron, *A Course of Love* (Take Heart Publications, 2014), 146.

2 Anthony De Mello, *Awareness* (Fount Paperbacks, 1990), 176.

3 bell hooks, *All About Love: New Visions* (William Morrow and Company Inc., 2018), Preface x.

4 Byron Katie, "Spotify Podcast: At Home with Byron Katie (podcast), July 27, 2020.

5 Gabor Maté, *The Myth of Normal: Trauma, Illness & Healing in a Toxic Culture,* (Avery, 2022), 20.

6 Oprah Winfrey and Bruce D. Perry, *What Happened to You?: Conversations on Trauma, Resilience and Healing,* (Flatiron Books, 2021).

7 Bessel van der Kolk, MD, *The Body Keeps The Score: Brain, Mind and Body in the Healing of Trauma* (Penguin Books, 2015).

8 Gary Zukav, "Occupy Your Heart," *Huffington Post*, March 31, 2012, https://www.huffpost.com/entry/occupy-your-heart_b_1241975.

9 Werner Erhard, "Responsibility," Werner Erhard Quotes (article), January 22, 2010, https://wernererhardquotes.wordpress.com/2010/01/22/responsibility.

10 Susan David, "Redefining Bravery: Courage is Not the Absence of Fear," Susan David (Newsletter) July 31, 2024. https://www.susandavid.com/newsletter/redefining-bravery-courage-is-not-the-absence-of-fear/.

11 Michel Gondry, "Dave Chappelle's Block Party," *Rogue Pictures*, (documentary), 103 minutes, September 12, 2005.

12 Byron Katie, *#174: He Wants to Date Other Women: The Work of Byron Katie*, Spotify (podcast), September 24, 2024, https://www.facebook.com/watch/?v=444027255346382.

13 Gregg Braden, *The Divine Matrix: Bridging Time, Space, Miracles, and Belief* (Hay House LLC, 2008).

14 "Do the best you can until you know better. Then when you know better, do better," attributed to Maya Angelou.

15 Sonya ReneeTaylor, *The Body Is Not an Apology: The Power of Radical Self-Love*. 2nd ed. (Berrett-Koehler Publishers, 2021).

16 Tricia Hersey, *Rest Is Resistance: A Manifesto*, First edition (Little, Brown Spark, 2022).

17 Katherine Woodward Thomas, *Calling In "The One"* (Harmony Books 2004, 2021)

18 Brené Brown, "Clear is Kind. Unclear is Unkind." Brené Brown (Blog) October 15, 2018, https://brenebrown.com/articles/2018/10/15/clear-is-kind-unclear-is-unkind/.

19 Julia Cameron, *The Artist's Way: A Spiritual Path to Higher Creativity* (Jeremy P. Tarcher/Perigee, 1992).

20 Tricia Hersey, *Rest Is Resistance: A Manifesto*. First edition (Little, Brown Spark, 2022).

21 Spencer Johnson, *Who Moved My Cheese?: An Amazing Way to Deal With Change in Your Work and in Your Life* (Putnam, 1998), 65.

22 Johnson, *Who Moved My Cheese?*, 45.

23 Martha Beck, *The Way of Integrity: Finding the Path of Your True Self* (Penguin Life, 2021).

24 Beck, *The Way of Integrity*.

25 Maya Angelou, *A Conversation with Maya Angelou*, BillMoyer.com (video), November 21, 1973, https://billmoyers.com/content/conversation-maya-angelou/.

26 Brené Brown, *Braving the Wilderness* (Vermilion, 2017).

27 1 Corinthians 13:11, New King James Version.

28 bell hooks, *All About Love: New Visions* (William Morrow and Company, Inc., 2018), 49.

29 Don Miguel Ruiz, *The Four Agreements* (Amber-Allen Publishing, 2001).

30 Desmond Tutu, Douglas Carlton, Abrams and Mpho A., Tutu, *The Book of Forgiving: The Fourfold Path for Healing Ourselves and Our World* (HarperOne, 2014).

31 Eleanor Roosevelt, *This Is My Story* (Harper, 1937).

32 Susan David, *Redefining Bravery: Courage is Not the Absence of Fear*, Susan David (Newsletter) July 31, 2024. https://www.susandavid.com/newsletter/redefining-bravery-courage-is-not-the-absence-of-fear/.

33 Don Miguel Ruiz, *The Four Agreements* (Amber-Allen Publishing, 2001).

34 Sharon Salzberg, *Real Love: The Art of Mindful Connection* (Flatiron Books, 2017).

35 Esther Perel, *Mating in Captivity: Reconciling the Erotic and the Domestic* (New York: HarperCollins, 2006).

36 Desmond Tutu, Douglas Carlton, Abrams and Mpho A., Tutu, *The Book of Forgiving: The Fourfold Path for Healing Ourselves and Our World* (HarperOne, 2014).

37 James Baldwin, *Nobody Knows My Name: More Notes of a Native Son* (Dial Press, 1961).

38 Sharon Salzberg, *Real Love: The Art of Mindful Connection* (Flatiron Books, 2017).

39 Katherine Woodward Thomas, *Conscious Uncoupling* (Harmony, 2015).

40 Henry Cloud and John Sims Townsend, *Boundaries: When to say yes, how to say no to take control of your life* (Zondervan, 2017).

41 "Caring for myself is not self-indulgence, it is self-preservation and that is an act of political warfare," attributed to Audre Lorde.

42 hooks, *All About Love*, Preface ix.

43 Adrian Gostick, "Harvard Research Reveals the #1 Key to Living Longer and Happier," *Forbes*, August 15, 2023, https://www.forbes.com/sites/adriangostick/2023/08/15/harvard-research-reveals-the-1-key-to-living-longer-and-happier/.

44 Louise Hay, "Louise Hay—Loving Yourself." YouTube. October 15, 2010. https://www.youtube.com/watch?v=Pq7BQydjYig.

45 Don Miguel Ruiz, *The Four Agreements* (Amber-Allen Publishing, 2001).

46 Andrea Hollingsworth, *What Chronic Self-criticism Does to Your Brain.* LinkedIn (article), April 19, 2023, https://www.linkedin.com/pulse/what-chronic-self-criticism-does-your-brain-hollingsworth-ph-d-/.

47 Sharon Salzberg, *Real Love: The Art of Mindful Connection* (Flatiron Books, 2017).

48 De Mello, *Awareness.*

49 Mirabai Bush and Ram Dass, *Walking Each Other Home: Conversations on Loving and Dying* (Avery, 2018).

50 "Time is a currency you can only spend once, so be careful how you spend it," attributed to Harmon Okinyo.

www.ingramcontent.com/pod-product-compliance
Lightning Source LLC
Chambersburg PA
CBHW031850200326
41597CB00012B/350